VITAL SIGNS—NEGATIVE

He was lying on the floor on his back, wearing a T-shirt and slacks but no shoes or socks. Fuehrer knelt beside him and felt for a pulse. Negative. Fuehrer felt for a heartbeat. Negative. He checked for other vital signs. Negative.

Lights were burning in the room, but not brightly enough for Fuehrer's purpose. He beamed a flashlight on the face. The eyes were partially open. Fuehrer could see a black spot surrounding a bullet hole over the left eye. When he checked the carotid artery, he spotted a hole in the neck. There were two more bullet holes—both behind the left ear. Blood was splashed on the floor and the nearest wall.

Although it hardly needed saying, Fuehrer nonetheless told Krause: "He's dead."

BLOOD
AND
REVENGE

**A True Story of Small-Town
Murder and Justice**

MICHAEL DORMAN

A DELL BOOK

Published by
Dell Publishing
a division of
Bantam Doubleday Dell Publishing Group, Inc.
666 Fifth Avenue
New York, New York 10103

ISBN: 0-440-20981-1

Printed in the United States of America

Published simultaneously in Canada

September 1991

10 9 8 7 6 5 4 3 2 1

OPM

For John Oliver—dedicated lawyer, devoted Texan, gracious gentleman, steadfast friend

Vengeance is in my heart, death
in my hand,
Blood and revenge are hammering
in my head.
—Shakespeare, *Titus Andronicus*

PROLOGUE

There was only the barest hint of a squeak when the downstairs doorknob turned at two-thirty in the morning. But it was enough to rouse Laraine Umstadter from sleep, and the next sound she heard was destined to send a chill surging straight to her soul.

"Mom!" came the frantic, anguished scream of her twenty-year-old son Travis. "Mom!" he shrieked again as he burst through the front door.

Now Travis was bounding up the stairs to the second floor, crying uncontrollably. "Oh, my God!" he said, sobbing. "Oh, my God! Mom! Mom!"

Laraine tumbled from the bed and ran to the second-floor landing, arriving at the same instant as Travis. Her husband, Dave, materialized silently beside her.

"What's wrong?" Laraine asked Travis. "What happened?"

But he merely continued to sob. "Oh, my God!" he said still again. "Oh, my God!"

Laraine, a small woman with a wispy fringe of blond bangs that lent an illusory sense of fragility to her oval face, seized her husky son by the shoulders and shook him hard. "Tell me what's wrong," she demanded.

Travis just stood there, weeping and shaking his head. Instinctively, Laraine led her son and her husband downstairs to the kitchen—the room reserved in their household for conversations of moment. She busied her hands, putting a pot of coffee on to brew.

Once more, she asked: "What happened?"

"I went to see Glenn Evans," Travis blurted at last. "I think he may be hurt."

Travis sank into a chair, cradled his head in his arms on the kitchen table, and cried so hard his entire body shuddered with great, heaving sobs. He could—or, at least, would—say no more for now.

Thus, Laraine Umstadter still did not know precisely what had happened. But from the little she had drawn from Travis, there were two points on which she could be certain. Whatever had happened out there in the darkness this night, it had been absolutely ghastly. And it had somehow involved her daughter, Kristen.

ONE

By the time she turned eighteen, Kristen Marie Umstadter had clearly carved out her place as the all-everything high school girl in Honesdale, Pennsylvania—a picturesque old railroad and resort town nestled among the gently undulating hills of the Pocono Mountains. Kristen not only had it all; she did it all.

She was the senior class president, an academic star, the homecoming queen, mainstay of the student council, a cross-country runner, the French Club president, a Sunday school teacher, and a founder of the local chapter of Students Against Drunk Driving. Bright, engaging, popular, ambitious, she was a beautiful blonde with sapphire eyes and deep dimples. One local official described her as "the kind of girl every father hopes his son will bring home someday."

How, then, it would later be asked, could such an altogether admirable young woman become the focal point of a succession of events that would bring cataclysm, vengeance, and murder descending on this pastoral little town?

How indeed?

Some saw what happened in Honesdale as a Shakespearean plot come to life. "It was kind of like the Montagues and the Capulets," said the local district attorney, Raymond Hamill. Surely, there was a certain Shakespearean inevitability to the tale. There was also a Shakespearean universality. The events could well have come to pass in any small town in America.

But they had actually come to pass in Honesdale—not without reason.

Honesdale (population, fifty-one hundred) is tucked in the far northeastern corner of Pennsylvania among magnificent pine and hardwood forests, scores of lakes, and a profusion of wildlife ranging from deer to black bear. In recent years both the town and surrounding Wayne County have witnessed the arrival of hundreds of new residents—many of them drawn by the area's natural beauty.

Thus it is common to hear townsfolk divide the citizenry into two groups: the natives and the transplants. When natives utter the word "transplant," at least a subtle hint of the pejorative can be discerned. Partly it results from a typical small-town wariness toward strangers. Partly it reflects resentment at seeing outlanders take over homes and property owned for generations by local families. And if the newcomers are perceived as "pushy" city folk, the resentment is likely to escalate by geometric proportions.

The Umstadters were regarded as transplants. It mattered not a whit that they had lived in Honesdale or its environs for more than a decade. Once a transplant, forever a transplant.

Dave Umstadter was born on December 17, 1941, in Paterson, New Jersey, his wife, eight months later, in Manhattan. Both grew up in New Jersey. They were high school sweethearts at Morris High in Bartley, a small town in the northwestern section of the state.

"We've been together since we were sixteen," Laraine is fond of saying. Two years out of high school, they were married in 1962. They made a sober, good-looking couple—Laraine fair with delicate features and wide-set blue eyes, Dave dark with high cheekbones and a square jaw.

By Laraine's description, Dave matured into "a jack of all trades and master of many." He made his living over the years as a farmer, a milkman, an automobile mechanic, the owner and driver of tractor-trailer rigs, and the proprietor of a prosperous general store.

Laraine, who would wait until middle age to become a college student and to pursue careers as a paralegal and a real-estate woman, gave birth to her first child the year after her marriage. He was named David Umstadter, Jr. Travis was born three years later. The year after that—on December 10, 1967—

Kristen was born at St. Clare's Hospital in Denville, New Jersey.

At least during their formative years, the Umstadter children were immersed in an environment so quintessentially all-American it bordered on cliché. First in New Jersey and later in Pennsylvania, they lived in a succession of unpretentious but comfortable homes out in the countryside. Their parents kept swarms of animals—horses, chickens, a cat called Kitty for Kristen, a dog called Lady for Travis. Kristen appointed herself the animals' keeper, playing with them, feeding them, caring for them, and going with them to the veterinarian at the slightest hint of trouble. Both she and her brothers adapted naturally to outdoor life, learning early such skills as skiing, snowmobiling, and woodsmanship. Travis began trapping and hunting animals while still a young boy.

Dave, Jr., mindful of the years separating him from his kid brother and sister, habitually went his own way. But Travis and Kristen, thrust together as playmates from infancy, became constant companions. As children they insisted on wearing identical clothing and copying each other's every mannerism and preference.

"They had to have the same color lollipops, the same sandwiches, the same everything," Laraine recalls. "I couldn't even give one of them a bath without giving the other a bath."

Laraine and Dave indulged them. And why not? They heard many other parents complaining about squabbling children. And here they were with a son and daughter who seemed genuinely crazy about each other. They counted that among their blessings.

When Travis was five, Laraine bought him a pair of cowboy boots. Before the boots even acquired their first scuff marks, Kristen asked: "Mom, can I have some boots just like those?" Of course she could. And as soon as she did, she and Travis went hiking in their new boots through the woods near their home. In the middle of the woods—not far from Lake Hopatcong, New Jersey—was a swamp. Naturally, nothing would do

but for Travis and Kristen to go trudging directly into the heart
of the swamp.

"Mom!" came two voices shouting as one. Laraine, back at
home, heard the shouts and followed the voices into the
swamp. She found Travis and Kristen stuck in the mud, unable
to move. Their boots were submerged in the muck. She first
lifted Kristen and then Travis out of the boots, carried them to
solid ground, then went back for the boots. It took days for the
boots to dry, and they were never the same. But somehow it
seemed fitting that when Travis and Kristen were forced to get
by with cruddy boots, the boots would be identically cruddy.

Not long afterward, Travis came upon an open can of paint
in the family's barn. "Let's paint the barn door," he told Kristen. They found a couple of paint brushes and began smearing
paint here and there on the door. But that soon lost its novelty.
Without warning or provocation, Travis suddenly flicked his
brush at Kristen and hit her in the face with a splat of paint.
Kristen retaliated with a flick and splat of her own. The Great
Paint War, as it would be called ever after in family lore, en-
sued. By the time a cease-fire was negotiated, both combatants
were covered top to toe in green paint. As for the barn, it was
red—except for the door, which had now become half red and
half green.

In June 1975, when Kristen was seven and Travis eight, the
Umstadters left New Jersey for Pennsylvania—moving into a
farmhouse about fifteen miles north of Honesdale in a cross-
roads community called Lookout. The countryside surrounding
Honesdale is dotted with dairy farms. Dave Umstadter tried
farming there for a time, but gave it up to buy the Lookout
General Store on State Highway 191—a rustic emporium long
popular not only with locals but also with outlanders who
flocked to the Honesdale area every hunting season.

By comparison with Honesdale—a small town but nonetheless the Wayne County seat and a modest mercantile center—
Lookout represented little more than a wide spot on a two-lane
road. Lookout was lumberjacket and flannel-shirt territory, a
natural habitat of the pickup truck, the scruffy beard, and the

occasional jaw stuffed with chewing tobacco. More than a few of the Lookout General Store's steady customers had, at one time or another, maintained at least a passing familiarity with the south end of a northbound mule.

Since there was no local elementary school, the Umstadter children rode a school bus forty-five minutes each way to the Preston School in the neighboring town of Damascus. From the start, teachers and administrators recognized Kristen as a prize student. She earned almost all A's, with no grade lower than B, in her first year—a record she would maintain from elementary school through high school. Her year-end evaluations throughout that entire period would be uniformly superlative, bearing not one critical word or suggestion for improvement.

At home, Kristen emerged as the unmistakable center of the Umstadter family's life. It was not simply that she was an over-achiever or the baby of the family or the only daughter. It was more than that, a case of her parents and brothers regarding her as their favorite person—loving, generous, bursting with life.

"I raised three kids," Laraine Umstadter says. "Kristen gave the most back." Another woman who watched Kristen grow up described her as "less than perfect but not much."

Kristen's brother Dave was the family clown—the wise-cracker, the kind of kid who would be characterized by a friend as "a piece of work." As for Travis, he was a piece of work as well. He was the one invariably enmeshed in some sort of mischief, usually nothing truly serious but sufficient to prompt his parents to shake their heads and wonder what would ever become of him.

When Travis was twelve, Laraine found a sealed condom inside the family clothes dryer while unloading a pile of wash. She had no doubt the item of evidence was traceable to Travis, for each of her children had an individual clothes hamper, and this load of wash had come solely from Travis's hamper. Laraine summoned Travis to her interrogation chamber—a small half-bathroom where she customarily ordered a suspect child to sit on the closed toilet seat while she stood with her back to the door, blocking the escape route, and fired questions.

"Do we have something to talk about?" Laraine asked.

"What?" Travis replied, the image of innocence.

"Don't ask me what. Tell me what this was doing in your wash." Laraine produced the evidence and thrust it at him.

"I got that at my friend David's birthday party," Travis said.

"You mean they were giving these out as party favors?"

"No, David just gave 'em to us."

"Where did he get them?"

"From his father's drawer."

After appropriate deliberation, Laraine released the suspect —deciding that he harbored no actual plan to make use of the evidence and that any punishment belonged in the jurisdiction of David's father.

Travis continued involving himself in minor scrapes after entering Honesdale High School in 1981. "He was a kid you'd like even though he could get himself in trouble," says Dan O'Neill, then the high school principal and now superintendent of schools. "He was a charming kid. He was good-looking. He liked girls, and girls liked him. When he was in trouble—say for coming to school late or something like that—you enjoyed talking to him. He always had some weird excuse he hoped would get him off the hook, and you couldn't help laughing at some of his stories."

Laraine concurs that Travis always had a story when in trouble, but she found his excuses far less amusing than O'Neill did. Typically, Travis would come rolling up to the house in his pickup truck late at night, long after the curfew established by his parents. Laraine would be waiting up for him.

"You missed your curfew," she would say. "Where were you?"

Then would come the story. One of Travis's favorites was: "I had truck trouble."

"Truck trouble?" Laraine would ask.

"Yeah, the truck wouldn't run. I had to get underneath it and fix it."

"That's funny," Laraine might say. "It's raining, and you didn't get the least bit wet or dirty. Come on, get your act together."

In high school, Travis was considered no more than an average student. "His grades weren't terrific but were okay," O'Neill says. "He was a tremendous underachiever, considering his intelligence. In some ways, he was very mature—seventeen going on twenty-five. He was a lineman on the football team through his junior year but gave it up in his senior year, probably because he just outgrew it. Travis outgrew some things because he was a little more mature than the other kids. He traveled in the fast lane a little bit. He'd have a few beers. He liked cars and girls and beer."

In truth, Travis liked beer a great deal. He particularly liked Genessee beer, a local favorite known in the vernacular as Genny. And he often drank more than just "a few." Travis began drinking when he was fourteen. Within a few years he was capable of downing two dozen bottles of beer—plus shots of apple schnapps—during a single extended drinking session.

At first, Dave and Laraine knew nothing about Travis's drinking. When they discovered it, they attempted repeatedly to persuade him to stop. But although he tried several times, he was soon drinking again.

All this drinking was illegal. The legal drinking age in Pennsylvania was twenty-one. Underage drinking, however, was no mere occasional aberration in the Honesdale area. Honesdale, not to mention Lookout, had little to offer teenagers in the way of entertainment. There was no movie house, nor even a bowling alley. Thus many teenagers passed their time hanging out illegally in bars or indulging in the custom known as cruising—driving the narrow, twisting mountain roads while belting down beer after beer. Travis had his own term for cruising. He would telephone one of his friends and ask: "Want to go on a road trip?" They would drive the back roads for hours, drinking and talking. Eventually Travis would wreck every truck and car he ever owned.

But the only trouble he encountered with the law over his

drinking involved a single bottle of beer. He took a summer job as a dishwasher at a restaurant and lounge called Kuester's in Beach Lake, a resort community just east of Honesdale. After work one night, Travis lingered for a beer. State liquor investigators, conducting a routine check, approached him and asked: "Can we see some ID?" They discovered he was underage and handed him a summons on a charge of illegal drinking.

To get the charge dismissed without standing trial, Travis agreed to enroll in a course on underage drinking. The course, taught by Wayne County's chief probation officer, Linus Myers, required attendance at five classes offered on consecutive nights. On one night each participant was obliged to bring one or both of his parents. "Usually, just one parent comes," Myers says. "But in Travis's case, both Laraine and Dave came. That impressed me. They seemed serious about helping him."

The course may have helped Travis temporarily, but soon he was drinking heavily again—perhaps not on week nights but just about every weekend by his senior year in high school. His entire family was concerned about him, Kristen most of all.

"She didn't agree with my drinking," Travis would later recall. "She used to try to talk to me about it. She wouldn't even ride in my car. She wouldn't come near me when I was drinking. She was totally against it."

By Kristen's junior year in high school she would often lie crying in bed while waiting for Travis to return from a night of drinking. The crying would sometimes begin even before he left.

One night, before going out, Travis asked Kristen: "Can you lend me some money? I'm broke."

Kristen stood there in torment, her chin quivering. The last thing she wanted to do was finance her brother's drinking. But she could not bear to deny him, either.

Tears cascaded down her face. She brushed at them with her hands, smudging her cheeks. At last she went to her purse, withdrew a twenty-dollar bill, and handed it to Travis.

"Be careful," she said, sobbing.

"Don't worry," he said.

Kristen lay awake for hours, crying, as she waited for Travis to come home. When he finally arrived, she emerged from her bedroom and called to him: "I'm glad you're home."

Travis shook his head and flashed her one of those indulgent half-smiles brothers reserve for kid sisters. "Go to bed," he said.

Travis's drinking represented a nagging enigma to Kristen and her parents. There was no history of heavy drinking in the family. Laraine and Dave took an occasional drink, but did not regularly have even a glass of wine with dinner. Nobody seemed able to explain why Travis should have such a problem and, since he denied there *was* a problem, the chance of a solution seemed remote.

It was Travis's drinking that prompted Kristen to become a founder of the Honesdale chapter of Students Against Drunk Driving. Every morning, shortly after Honesdale radio station WDNH went on the air, Kristen's soft, singsong voice could be heard broadcasting a taped SADD appeal to listeners. "Friends don't let friends drive drunk," she would say.

Kristen campaigned relentlessly against drinking and driving, organizing parties and other activities intended to demonstrate that it was possible for teenagers to have a good time without alcohol. When Wayne County responded to Nancy Reagan's "Just Say No" campaign by organizing a task force on drug and alcohol abuse, Kristen was named to the group as SADD's representative.

And when community leaders conducted a public forum on alcohol and narcotics, Kristen was the only teenager chosen for the speakers' panel. She emphasized students could find an abundance of kicks without resorting to drink or drugs.

"I get high on life," she said.

Her own life at the time, except for concern over Travis, seemed luminous. Oh, there were a few changes she would have made—chiefly concerning her appearance—if granted the power. As beautiful as she was, she nonetheless engaged in a never-ending search for flaws.

She was obsessed with the notion that her thighs were heavy

and ugly. Actually, they were neither heavy nor ugly but just the normally muscular thighs of a cross-country runner. But Kristen would complain constantly that she was afflicted with thunder thighs. "You've got chicken legs," she would tell Laraine. "So how come I've got thunder thighs?" Kristen also harbored the illusion that her legs were unusually hairy. She shaved them incessantly, needed or not. Even one of her more stunning characteristics—her naturally curly, dark blond hair —failed to suit her. Prevailing styles notwithstanding, she wanted straight hair.

Still, aside from such irritants, Kristen seemed at peace with herself. She was earning her usual high grades at Honesdale High. She had been elected junior class president, was serving her third year on the student council, and was on her way to winning her letter on the cross-country team. To earn spending money, she was working part-time as a waitress at the Towne House Diner on Honesdale's Main Street—a popular fourteen-booth, fourteen-stool establishment where townsfolk mixed sustenance with gossip and the decor mixed chrome with Formica. Conveniently, a high school friend of Kristen's, Lorraine Cush, also worked there. During slack periods the two girls would pass the time in casual chitchat while wiping the counter endlessly, filling the salt shakers, and replacing empty ketchup bottles.

Fred Chalmers, a tall, slender transplant from Long Island who operates the diner, initially had reservations about hiring Kristen. "In this business, I've learned that it's not always smart to hire pretty girls," Chalmers says. "Many of them just stand around, looking pretty, and let everyone else do the work. But Kristen was never that way. She'd get right down on her hands and knees and scrub the place spotless. She worked here for a year, and the customers loved her. It wasn't just her cute little turned-up nose or her cute little turned-up bosom. Everybody could see she was a wonderful girl. She could have served the customers gruel and they would have asked for more, given her a big tip, and come back again soon."

Kristen used part of her earnings from the diner to augment

her wardrobe. She was as particular about her appearance as about her schoolwork, favoring a look she considered feminine but not frilly—button-down blouses (often in lavender, her favorite color), western skirts, cowboy boots, jeans. To enhance that look, she studied makeup techniques at a grooming school in Wilkes-Barre. She was forever painting her fingernails and toenails. And she huffed, puffed, jumped, twisted, and stretched her way daily through the Jane Fonda exercise program. Her natural good looks and all this attention to her appearance brought occasional modeling opportunities. On one assignment, she posed in a bridal gown—with Honesdale mayor Richard Kreitner playing the father of the bride—for pictures used to promote a local photography studio.

Although she looked entirely believable in the bridal pictures, Kristen had yet to become involved in even a serious romance—much less to contemplate actually wearing a wedding gown of her own. She had begun dating only when she turned sixteen, during her sophomore year. For months, beginning when she was seventeen, she went out with a boy named Danny Soden, who played on the football team and was the class vice president. Some called them "the two straightest kids in the high school." That common outlook, however, was not enough to sustain a romance. They eventually decided to be just friends. Kristen then dated several other boys, but enduring attachments were yet to come.

"Kristen did so many things so well that some boys would shy away from her," says high school principal Dan O'Neill. "They were a little intimidated by her, even though she never tried to intimidate anyone. In fact, far from closing herself off in some elite group, she made it a point to travel in two circles —the overachievers and the others. It was important to her to be accepted by both groups."

In June 1985, when Kristen completed her junior year, Travis received his diploma from Honesdale High. Asked by the yearbook editors to describe his long-range ambition, Travis replied: "To survive." That was it. Travis did not know what he wanted to do with his life. He spoke vaguely to friends of becoming a long-haul driver of tractor-trailer rigs. But for the short term, he took a job as a carpenter. The work involved, in the local jargon, "framing houses"—erecting the wooden frames for homes being built chiefly to accommodate the current crop of newly arriving transplants.

In his spare time, aside from hanging out and drinking with his friends, Travis continued to hunt and trap. He laid numerous traps for small game in the woods near the Umstadter home. Occasionally he would find an animal snared in one of his traps but still alive. He would return home, borrow a .25-caliber automatic pistol Laraine kept in a night table, and use it to kill the animal.

On Christmas Day of 1985, when the Umstadters gathered around the tree to open their presents, Travis was handed a heavy package by his father. "What's this?" Travis asked.

"Open it," Dave said.

Travis tore the wrapping paper from the package. Inside, he found a gun of his own—a gold-etched .22-caliber revolver with a six-inch barrel. The gun, manufactured by Excam, Inc. of Hialeah, Florida, was fitted with a single-action firing mechanism. Thus it would not fire consecutive bullets if someone simply squeezed the trigger again and again. A shooter would have to perform two steps—first pulling back the hammer with his thumb, then squeezing the trigger—for each shot.

Travis later took the revolver out and test-fired a few rounds, checking the single-action mechanism. Pull, squeeze. Pull, squeeze. Pull, squeeze. After reloading the gun with six Remington cartridges, he slid it beneath the driver's seat of his car to keep it close at hand.

He never knew when he might need it.

TWO

Kristen Umstadter's senior year at Honesdale High School was pure gold—all she had ever hoped it might be. She was elected senior class president. She served still another year on the student council. She was crowned homecoming queen before a roaring throng of spectators at the year's biggest football game, then presided over a long weekend celebration that did not end until the last tiny lick of flame had died in Honesdale High's traditional bonfire.

Beyond all that, Kristen could see her plans for the years ahead falling securely into place. Although she had applied to several colleges, her first choice was to study horticulture at Temple University in Philadelphia—a three-hour drive south of Honesdale. Her guidance counselor, Carl Cerar, urged Temple to accept her. "Kristen is a first-class student," Cerar said in one letter to the university's admissions officers. "She is not afraid to assume a strong leadership role, bringing organization, courtesy, and success to all tasks. She has academic ability, which enables her to succeed in school. All her teachers report she is a sure bet for success."

Temple not only accepted her but also granted her a scholarship. She would be expected on campus for the fall semester of 1986.

As much respect as Kristen's accomplishments engendered, there were some—parents and students alike—who attributed her success largely to pressure from her mother. This talk drifted back to Laraine and infuriated her. "I've heard people say I pushed Kristen in high school," she says. "It's just not so. What Kristen did in high school wasn't parent-directed. It was peer-directed. Being president of the senior class, I had nothing to do with that. She was elected to that. Being homecoming queen, she was elected to that. I didn't have anything to do with that. Everything she did in high school she did on her own."

Whatever was driving her, Kristen seemed ubiquitous during that senior year—scurrying from class to class at the high school, organizing student activities, running mile after mile at cross-country practice, baby-sitting for neighbors, holding down a part-time job, teaching Sunday school at the local Presbyterian church. With her usual intensity, she continued to crusade against alcohol both individually and through her work with Students Against Drunk Driving.

Immediately after the senior prom each year, it was the custom for Honesdale High students to prolong the festivities by gathering for private parties where at least some drank themselves to the fringes of catatonia. Not infrequently, there were drunk-driving accidents on the way home.

For her prom, Kristen mounted a small, private revolution against the prevailing custom. She organized an alcohol-free breakfast following the dance. At 2:30 A.M., fourteen of her friends gathered at the Umstadter home to continue the night's revelry. Raucous they may have been, but under the influence they were not. The strongest beverage served was hot coffee.

Laraine Umstadter would recall, however, that one incident had marred the breakfast: At 5:30 A.M., a young friend of Kristen's named Heidi Stacier had shown up at the Umstadter home—sick and displaying obvious signs that she had been drinking.

If one void existed in Kristen's life at the time, it was the absence of romance. Although she dated often, she still had no serious boyfriend. But she did have her eye on a prospect.

His name was Allan Rutledge. He had been a part of Kristen's life almost as long as she could remember. They had met in the fifth grade, attending the same class at the Preston School and riding the school bus together. Allan, who had lived all of his eighteen years on his parents' farm in the Wayne

County community of Tyler Hill, had grown up as a close friend of Travis Umstadter's—even though Travis was a year ahead of him in school.

Over the years, Allan and Travis had raised all kinds of hell together. One Halloween, they bought several cartons of eggs, rode to a local shopping center in Travis's pickup truck, bombarded sundry teenagers and their vehicles, then fled with two truckloads of furious pursuers on their tail. Travis, familiar with every road in the county, turned off U.S. Highway 6 south of Honesdale, then raced down a bewildering succession of back roads that Allan did not even know existed. But they were unable to shake the trucks following them.

Travis jammed on the brakes and stopped. He and Allan jumped from the pickup, egged their victims a second time, and took off again down the road. One pursuing truck dropped out of the chase, but the other stayed within closing range.

"Let's stop and take 'em on," Allan urged.

"Don't worry about it," Travis said. "They'll never make the next curve."

Travis swerved around a hairpin turn, drove another hundred yards, and pulled off the road near a grove of hemlocks. "If they make the curve, we'll take 'em on here," Travis said. "But they'll never make it."

The driver of the pursuing truck spotted the curve far too late. He floored the brakes, skidded sideways, and slammed into a tree. Travis and Allan turned around, drove back to the tree, and determined that nobody was hurt but the truck was on the critical list. Mercilessly, they pelted the truck's occupants with still more eggs, then drove off into the night.

As Allan Rutledge and Travis Umstadter had learned long before, Halloween in Honesdale was not Parcheesi.

By the time Allan became a high school senior along with Kristen Umstadter, he had grown into a handsome, black-haired boulder of a young man—six-feet-four and 225 pounds of muscle and bone. Although he stood almost a foot taller than Kristen, it often occurred to him that he had spent much of his life looking up to *her*. She was everything he had ever wanted, but he had always been afraid to approach her even for a date—much less any sort of long-term commitment. She was just too perfect, he feared, to get involved with the likes of him. Besides, she was Travis's sister. Besides, whenever he thought he might dredge up the nerve to ask for a date, she seemed to be going out with someone else. Besides . . .

Yet, Kristen and Allan did spend a good deal of time together. Kristen's brother Dave operated a video shop on Highway 191, not far from their father's general store. Kristen would bring movies home from the shop and show them to small gatherings of friends. Usually Allan would be among those invited. But somehow he and Kristen never seemed to find themselves alone; they were always surrounded by others.

Then, one frosty March day in 1986, Kristen invited Allan to her home. He assumed some of their friends would be there as well. But he found only Kristen.

As she would eventually confess: "I wanted to get you alone."

They laughed. They talked. They listened to country-and-western music.

After an interminable inner struggle, Allan mustered the courage to ask: "How about going out with me sometime?"

"Sure," Kristen said. "I'd like that."

"You know, I've always wanted to go out with you," Allan told her. "But you always seemed to be going with someone else or something."

"Well, I've always wanted to go out with *you*. But *you* always seemed to be going with someone else."

And so it began—a small-town teenage romance in the classic tradition. The dates were scarcely elaborate. Allan and Kristen would watch movies, just the two of them, at the Umstadter home. They would ride around in Allan's blue Chevrolet pickup, listening to music on the radio. Kristen, unabashedly romantic, would search the dial for love songs. She would listen endlessly to the music of the country-and-western band Alabama—the big 1986 hit called "Touch Me When We're Dancing" and such earlier numbers as "When We Make

Love" and "Love in the First Degree." But her all-time favorite
song was Canadian rock star Bryan Adams's "Summer of '69'.

In the right mood, riding along with Allan in his truck, Kristen would sing along when a familiar song came over the radio.
That is not to say she could carry the tune. Kristen had many
talents, but musical gifts were not among them. She had once
taken piano lessons, with negligible results. The musical ability
in the family had been bestowed—some said wasted—on
Travis. He had a rich baritone voice but would rarely permit
anyone to hear it. And he was a skilled pianist but stopped
playing because he considered the talent somehow unmascu-
line. Kristen did not share Travis's inhibitions. She would sing
or occasionally play the piano, with zest if not distinction.

As young romantics will, Kristen and Allan conjured up
their own private little world in which the most mundane acts,
previously performed by God knows how many generations of
teenagers, somehow seemed freshly invented just for them.
Holding hands in the pickup—refusing to let go even when the
gears on the standard transmission needed shifting or the steering wheel needed turning—they behaved as if they were the
only two sweethearts on earth ever to confront such circumstances. Occasionally they ran off the road. Once they barely
missed a collision. Each time, although fully cognizant of the
danger, they just laughed and drove on with their hands still
entwined.

Allan would take his eyes from the road now and then during their travels to look over at Kristen. Often she would be
sitting there with her face close to his—staring at him with
what he took to be an expression of sheer adoration. That was
something new for him.

In fact, much was new for him in this romance. Although he
was in many ways a worldly young man, he had spent most of
his life in a closely constricted area generally confined to the
northern section of Wayne County near his family's farm. Kristen opened his eyes to distant places with accounts of trips she
had made—annual visits with grandparents in Charlottesville,
Virginia, ski trips to Vermont, vacation travels with friends to

Florida and North Carolina. Closer to home, Kristen introduced Allan to places he had never visited on his own.

The most popular recreation attraction nearby is Lake Wallenpaupack, eleven miles south of Honesdale. Created in 1925 by damming a creek for an enormous hydroelectric project, Lake Wallenpaupack is the largest man-made body of water in Pennsylvania—thirteen miles long, with fifty-two miles of shoreline, depths reaching sixty feet, and a capacity of seventy billion gallons. All this water is surrounded by acre upon acre of dense evergreen forests. Thousands of vacationers flock to the lake every year, many from far-off states.

Yet, Allan Rutledge had never been to Lake Wallenpaupack until Kristen Umstadter took him there one night. They walked along the beach, holding hands and stopping here and there to kiss. The lake soon became their special place, as if they held exclusive beach rights to the rituals of young love.

One evening in May, two months after they began dating, they were strolling the beach holding hands when Allan abruptly turned to Kristen and asked: "How about going steady?"

Kristen stopped walking. She grinned, threw her arms around Allan, stood on tiptoes, and gently kissed him. "You know the answer," she said.

They pursued all the requisite conventions. Allan gave Kristen his high school ring—many sizes too large for her. She wound yarn inside the ring so it would fit her finger. Kristen gave Allan her school ring. Since there was no way it would fit any of his fingers, he wore it on a chain around his neck.

Honesdale's main shopping mall, the Route 6 Plaza, stands on the west side of U.S. 6 at the southern end of town. Kristen was working at the time for an appliance store, Vanderwell Sales, at the mall. Coincidentally but conveniently, Allan was working at a Mobil station just across the highway. During slack times they would peer at each other or wave greetings. Occasionally they would talk on the telephone—each within sight and shouting distance of the other. For them, if not for some teenagers, it seemed infinitely more discreet to whisper "I love you" into a telephone than to shout it across a federal highway.

Neither Allan nor Kristen knew where their romance was going. Allan, for his part, was not certain where his life was going. Although bright and articulate, he did not think college was for him. He hoped for a career in business, but felt he could pursue it without a college education.

Thus he had committed himself to a hitch in the Navy after finishing high school. He was to take eight weeks of basic training at the Great Lakes naval base in Illinois, then return home for an extended leave before reporting to the submarine base at New London, Connecticut. By the time he came home on leave, Kristen was scheduled to be off to college. But Philadelphia was close enough so that they could see each other, whether Allan was at home or in New London.

Still, when they talked it over not long after their graduation with Honesdale High's Class of '86, they decided to put the romance on hold while Allan was in basic training. Each would be free to date others during that time. But the understanding was that they would resume the romance when Allan came home on leave after two months. While he was gone, they would write each other daily and talk occasionally by phone.

Kristen kept Allan's school ring, as well as a locket he had given her. But he returned her ring for safekeeping, since he would not be permitted to wear it in the Navy. On July 23, after an emotional farewell at which they renewed the pledge to write every day, Allan left for Great Lakes.

They did write every day. The trouble was that, for some curious reason, the mail initially did not get through in either direction. After more than ten days, Kristen had not received one letter. Nor had Allan. Both were frantic. Then, on the same day, each received a week's worth of mail—bursting with assurances of enduring love. The romance might be on hold, but it was unquestionably alive.

Kristen busied herself during the summer with the chores necessary to prepare for college—getting her clothes ready, buying supplies, having her car checked. Her parents had bought her a 1981 Honda to take to Philadelphia, replacing the overhauled 1970 Camaro she had been driving.

Laraine Umstadter saw signs of increasing maturity in her daughter. Some of these signs might have seemed trivial to outsiders, but Laraine considered them significant nonetheless. Kristen wore reading glasses, and Laraine had always taken her to the optometrist's office to order them. One day that summer, Kristen asked: "Mom, how about taking me to get new glasses?"

"You don't need me to go with you to buy glasses," Laraine told her. "Go down there and do it yourself."

Apparently the thought had never occurred to Kristen. But she went down, picked out the frames, was fitted for lenses, and placed the order. To Laraine, that simple event—contemplated alongside others of its kind—provided clear evidence that "Kristen wasn't a teenybopper anymore."

Recognizing that maturity, Laraine encouraged Kristen to spread her wings still wider. But there were always limits. As the summer wore on, a close friend of Kristen's—a young man named Chris Mott—invited her to fly with him to California for a visit with relatives. Kristen wanted to go, and Chris asked Laraine if that would be all right. Laraine's initial inclination was to say yes. Then she heard the kicker: Although the two teenagers would fly to California, the plan called for them to drive back—at a leisurely two-week pace, no less.

"The two of you on the road together for two weeks?" Laraine asked incredulously. "No way!"

Chris made the trip. Kristen did not. She faced a full agenda at home, in any event, before leaving for college. The Umstadter family was building a large new modern house in an area called Duck Harbor Pond north of Honesdale. Travis and his father were doing much of the work themselves. While the new house was under construction, the family moved temporarily from Lookout to a home in Honesdale proper. Kristen and all the Umstadters spent days making the move and getting settled in the Honesdale home.

It was a white and yellow, two-story frame house perched

high on a hill at 252 Erie Street. The front windows looked down on Honesdale's largest industrial enterprise—the Moore Business Forms plant, employing more than a thousand workers and producing ton upon ton of materials required to perpetuate America's annual paperwork blizzard. On the front of the house was a small open porch, with a door leading into the living room and the adjoining kitchen and dining room. Upstairs were the master bedroom, a second room for Kristen, and a third shared by Travis and Dave, Jr. Kristen's room was bright and pink—pink carpeting, a profusion of pink roses in the wallpaper, and other splashes of pink here and there.

One day in early August, while Kristen was working at the appliance store in the mall, a young man named Glenn Evans struck up a conversation. Slender, large-featured, with long, dark hair, Glenn was about to turn twenty and had gone through high school with Travis Umstadter. They were not close friends—merely two of the more than two hundred members of their graduating class—but they did know each other casually. After a bit of small talk, Glenn asked Kristen to go to the Wayne County Fair with him the following Sunday. Kristen said she would have to let him know.

Since she knew little about Glenn, she wanted to check him out. Later, at home, Travis pronounced his judgment. "Glenn's okay," he said. "He's not too bright, but he's okay."

Opinions of Glenn elsewhere in Honesdale were mixed. Some said he was wild, that he drank heavily, drove recklessly, and persistently chased younger girls. But others described him as self-reliant, hardworking, a kid who had done well for himself considering the hard times he had endured.

There was no question Glenn had grown up surrounded by adversity. He was born in Scranton, about thirty miles southwest of Honesdale, into a family with six other children. His parents, John and Eva Evans, were divorced while he was a child—his father settling in Dalton, Pennsylvania, his mother in Cochecton, New York, just across the state line from Honesdale. Glenn bounced around as a child, staying sometimes with one of his parents, at other times with an older brother's family.

His mother suffered a succession of misfortunes after the divorce. First, she was badly burned leaping from a flaming house in which her boyfriend and his two children burned to death. Two years later, she was left a paraplegic by an automobile accident on an icy road. Now, Glenn was sharing an apartment with an older brother, Mark, in a converted barn just outside Honesdale.

Glenn was one of those kids crazy about cars. He drove them relentlessly, he occasionally smacked them up, he repaired them, he repainted them, and, if he found them worthy, he revered them. At the time he encountered Kristen in the appliance store, he was enrolled as an automotive-mechanics student at Johnson Technical Institute in Scranton.

Had Kristen asked high school principal Dan O'Neill's opinion of Glenn—which she had not—she would have been told that Glenn and Travis were so similar O'Neill regarded them as clones. "If you asked me while they were in high school about seven characteristics of young men that age, Travis and Glenn would have had at least five characteristics that were identical," O'Neill says. "Both were in-the-middle kids. Their grades were in the middle. They were neither liberal nor conservative—just middle-of-the-road. They were both good kids. They both liked a beer. They had about the same temperaments, although Travis's temper was a little hotter than Glenn's."

Leaning back in a chair in his Spartan office, O'Neill falls silent for a few moments, runs his right hand through his close-cropped gray hair, and grasps for a succinct way to characterize these two young men during their student days. Upon reflection, it comes to him.

"They were both the kind of kids who, if they live to age twenty-five, wind up becoming solid citizens," he says.

THREE

Glenn Evans screeched to a stop, burning rubber, when he drove up to the Umstadter home on Erie Street to collect Kristen for their date at the county fair. He was polite enough during the introductions to Laraine and Dave Umstadter. But then, as Glenn rode off with Kristen in his red 1971 Plymouth Duster, he gunned the motor and sent gravel flying across the street—a performance, all in all, not particularly inclined to score points with a new date's doting parents.

It was Sunday, August 10, 1986, the last day of the 124th annual Wayne County Fair. Glenn and Kristen rode through downtown Honesdale, then north for a mile on Highway 191 to the fairgrounds. They parked in a pasture and picked their way through mounds of cow manure to the entrance.

Before them sat a big, old wooden grandstand painted barn red, with a green shingled roof. Beneath the stands were booths where a fairgoer could obtain a palm reading, stoke up on kielbasa or pierogi or pizza or Italian sausage or ice cream, shop from a selection of hundreds of hunting knives, buy a device designed to keep eyeglasses from slipping down the nose, get an electronic handwriting analysis, or hear a pitch on behalf of the Chamber of Commerce, the Honesdale Church of Christ, or Lackawanna Junior College.

Out in back of the grandstand stood the traditional array of amusement concessions—the fun house, giant slide, bumper cars, Ferris wheel, train ride, skee ball, bingo, and a game called frog bog in which players tried to catapult rubber frogs onto simulated lily pads by slamming down a heavy mallet. Kristen and Glenn strolled the midway, stopping here and there to try a ride or game.

Along the way, Kristen encountered Allan Rutledge's brother, Bruce. They stopped only long enough for an awkward exchange of hellos. The next day, in her regular letter to Allan, Kristen would casually refer to attending the fair with Glenn. "I guess she figured she'd better mention it because she'd run into my brother," Allan would later conclude.

The main action at the fair was played out in the arena set before the grandstand. There, during the previous six days, fairgoers had witnessed the judging of cattle, swine, sheep, and poultry, the auction of baked goods, and the woodsmen's competition (tree felling, chain-sawing huge logs, tree climbing, log rolling). But now the chief attraction—certainly the one of greatest interest to Glenn Evans—was a huge demolition derby.

Glenn and Kristen found seats high in the grandstand. As a member of the local car-worshiping fraternity, Glenn knew many of the drivers competing in the derby. They all hung out at the same garages and beer joints. It was another milieu in which Glenn and Travis Umstadter crossed paths. Travis occasionally raced stock cars at White Lakes Raceway, across the New York State line about ten miles from Lookout.

Crash! The mayhem began with an old Dodge jalopy smashing into the right side of a Ford. Bang! A rear-ender. Crunch! A carom shot—a Chevy slamming a Chrysler into a Plymouth. Bam! Clang! Kaboom!

Smoke and dust drifted into the darkened sky. Every collision produced a roar from the grandstand. The greatest roar was reserved for the decisive moment when only one battered car—civilized society's contemporary representation of a triumphant gladiator, lacking only the sword—remained capable of moving about the littered arena under its own power.

Glenn loved it. As for Kristen, she had never been crazy about the destructive violence inherent in demolition derbies. But she did seem to enjoy watching Glenn have a good time.

When Glenn drove Kristen home that night, he again burned rubber outside her home. Dave Umstadter mentioned to Laraine that he did not like the way Glenn drove. But neither of Kristen's parents did or said anything intended to prevent her from going out with Glenn again. They did not expect Kristen to become involved in any serious romance with him. "I just thought she felt sorry for Glenn because he'd had a hard life," Laraine would recall.

It was Wednesday night, August 13. Kristen came home from work at the appliance store carrying a batch of strawberries and a container of cream. Glenn was celebrating his twentieth birthday, and she had decided to bake him a cake. She had checked with his brother Mark and learned that Glenn had not had a birthday cake since he was a child, but that his favorite was vanilla cake with strawberries and whipped cream. Kristen needed no help baking the cake. She had been cooking and baking since she was a young girl. Often, if she had nothing else to do on a Sunday afternoon, she would suggest to Laraine: "Let's bake something." When she finished baking Glenn's cake, Kristen drove to his apartment, gave it to him, and stayed long enough to join in a brief celebration.

It was Friday, August 15. Kristen returned from work about 7:00 P.M. and changed clothes—putting on gray jeans, a white sweatshirt with a V design down the front, and a pair of new sneakers. She was wearing pearl earrings, her high school ring, and the locket Allan Rutledge had given her.

Kristen planned to spend part of the evening dropping by to see friends and giving them the Philadelphia address where they could reach her once she left for college. Laraine had typed the address on recipe cards for her. Two of Kristen's friends, Lorraine Cush and Heidi Stacier, had agreed to go with her.

Lorraine, who had worked with Kristen at the Towne House Diner, was eighteen, but there was a worldly air about her that made her seem older. She had been a cheerleader for the high school sports teams, the Honesdale Hornets, and looked the part—slender, long-legged, sandy-haired, full of energy. Like Kristen, Lorraine had taken part in a multitude of extracurricular activities. Also like her, she had been a good student. She had been accepted for the fall semester at Duquesne University in Pittsburgh.

Heidi, the girl Laraine Umstadter recalled as showing up under the influence at Kristen's alcohol-free breakfast the night of the senior prom, was slim and dark-haired. She was only sixteen, so it was understandable that she would seem conspicuously less mature than the two other girls. While Kristen and Lorraine would soon be starting college, Heidi would be entering the eleventh grade. She was considered an average student. Since she worked long hours at a succession of after-school jobs, Heidi took little part in extracurricular activities. She lived not far from the Umstadters, in a house on Honesdale's Park Street, with her mother and her stepfather, John Sherwood, the administrator of Wayne County Memorial Hospital.

Lorraine, Heidi, and Kristen were not particularly close friends. Kristen's mother, in fact, considered them mere "school acquaintances." Moreover, she had her reservations about Heidi and Lorraine—Heidi because of the prom-night episode, Lorraine because of another incident said to involve drinking. Kristen had told her mother that Lorraine had once tried persistently to coax her into drinking at a party, even though her opposition to alcohol was well known.

Still, Kristen did want to see Lorraine and Heidi before she went off to college. So she had made arrangements to spend this Friday night with them.

About seven-thirty, Kristen picked up Heidi at her home. They then rode to Kristen's bank, where she cashed a paycheck she had received earlier in the day.

Lorraine Cush, who had told Kristen she would meet her at the Umstadter home, arrived there before Kristen returned with Heidi. Lorraine mentioned to Laraine Umstadter that she had been working at a local swimming pool during the summer and was now qualified to teach courses in cardiopulmonary resuscitation. If Kristen were interested, Lorraine said, she could help her qualify for a Red Cross CPR card before the fall college semester began.

When Kristen returned, Laraine Umstadter said: "Lorraine just told me she can give you a crash CPR course before you go to school."

"Really?" Kristen replied.

And then, without another word, the girls were bustling out the door to Kristen's Honda. They drove off, delivered a few of the address cards, then rode up and down Main Street for a half-hour and discussed what to do next.

What they actually decided to do next was drive to Kuester's, the restaurant and lounge in nearby Beach Lake where Travis Umstadter had formerly worked as a dishwasher. They stayed at Kuester's only about five minutes. When they drove away, they took with them two six-packs of Michelob Light beer. They then returned to Honesdale and cruised the town— drinking the beer and stopping here and there to talk to friends.

Kristen Umstadter, the adamant crusader against drinking and driving, the radio voice of Students Against Drunk Driving, cruising around and swigging from a bottle of beer? Some, including her parents, would never believe it. Others, who might believe it, would never understand it. Yet the available evidence indicates it happened. And that's not all that happened.

It was nine-thirty. The girls stopped for hamburgers at the local McDonald's restaurant on Highway 6 near the shopping mall. They then drove to the headquarters of the Honesdale ambulance corps, where they talked for a few minutes with several of Heidi's friends.

It was almost ten o'clock. The girls were again pondering what to do next. "Let's go see Glenn," Kristen suggested. Lorraine and Heidi had no better idea, so off they went. Kristen followed Highway 6 north and then west into the community of Seelyville, on the outskirts of Honesdale. At the intersection of Township Route 472, she turned right, then right again into a parking lot behind a brown wooden structure known as the Buckley Building—once a barn but now a two-story apartment house.

Kristen knocked at the door of Apartment Three. Glenn Evans came to the door and ushered the girls into the living room. He had a bottle of Michelob in his hand. The girls brought their own beer with them. To Heidi, Glenn seemed drunk. His eyes were bloodshot. His hair was a mess. His clothing was a mess.

Glenn *had* been drinking beer for more than four hours by the time the girls arrived. He had ridden to Scranton and back earlier in the evening with a friend, Mark Ordnung, and the two of them had finished most of a twelve-pack during the round-trip. Glenn continued drinking beer after he returned home. Ordnung was still with him when the girls came to the apartment.

Music was blaring from a radio. Glenn and Kristen sat on a couch and tried to talk above the noise. Lorraine, from what she could hear, concluded they were having "a little bit of a spat." Glenn seemed irritated because Kristen had told him earlier she was staying home for the evening, but now here she was on his doorstep at ten o'clock. Heidi, for her part, drew the impression that Glenn did not want the girls there.

Kristen and Glenn went outside for perhaps twenty minutes. Heidi and Lorraine played darts to pass the time. When Kristen returned, she told Heidi: "Glenn's acting like a jerk."

It was ten-fifty. Heidi was getting bored. She drew Kristen aside in the kitchen and said she wanted to leave. "I'll take you home," Kristen told the younger girl.

Everyone went outside. Mark Ordnung drove away in his car. But Kristen, instead of entering her Honda, unexpectedly told Heidi and Lorraine: "We're going for a ride in Glenn's car."

The four of them piled into the red Duster—Glenn at the wheel, Kristen in the bucket seat beside him, Heidi behind her, and Lorraine in the left rear. Glenn had an open bottle of beer wedged between his thighs as he drove. Lorraine and Heidi were sharing a bottle. Several other bottles of beer, which Glenn had carried to the car in a paper bag, were perched on the console between Glenn and Kristen.

Again, it all seemed incongruous. Kristen, the leader of SADD, going for a ride with a driver who had been "acting like a jerk," had been drinking for hours, and now had a bottle of beer between his thighs? Incongruous or not, it was happening.

Glenn pulled onto Route 6 with a rush and a skid. The car spun and fishtailed across the road. Glenn straightened it out, then took off along the winding, two-lane road toward Honesdale at high speed, swinging wide on the turns—the left side of his car encroaching across the center line. When he reached Honesdale, he drove south along Main Street with his left wheels still across the center line. A northbound car was headed straight at him. Its driver honked insistently, and Glenn moved to the right. Just outside the gate to the Moore Business Forms plant near Kristen's home, Glenn turned left and headed toward Beach Lake.

At that moment, in Beach Lake, a young woman named Stacy Scheuren and her boyfriend, Michael Madan, were celebrating at Kuester's. Stacy, twenty-two, had learned earlier in the day that she was being hired to teach school in Narrowsburg, just across the New York State line.

Michael and Stacy were looking for several friends who were supposed to join them for the celebration. But Kuester's—a sprawling roadhouse adorned with pictures of Herman's Hermits, the Shirelles, and other performers who had played there over the years—was swarming with Friday-night revelers, and neither Stacy nor Michael had thus far been able to spot the friends in the crowd.

At the same time, a man named V. A. Conrad, who lived near Beach Lake, was out with his eleven-year-old daughter, Kerstin, for a late ice-cream stop. Kerstin lived in Georgia with Conrad's former wife but was making a custody visit with her father.

Glenn Evans did not drive all the way to Beach Lake. After heading south to the community of Indian Orchard, he turned east at a hot-dog eatery called Mustard's Last Stand and headed up Highway 652—a narrow, hilly, winding road that passes through Beach Lake on its way to Narrowsburg. Weaving in and out of traffic, passing cars in no-passing zones, slugging now and then at his bottle of beer, he raced at speeds reaching eighty miles an hour past dairy farms, automobile repair shops, and an enormous field filled with hulks of old earth-moving machines.

As he drove, Glenn leaned periodically to his right across the console and kissed Kristen. At times, not alone when Glenn was engaged in such contortions, his car would hit the dirt shoulder on its right and bump along until he could maneuver back to the pavement. At other times the car would again drift to the left across the center line. Once, at least, Kristen grabbed the steering wheel and pulled it to the right to turn the car back into its own lane. Shortly before the car would have reached Beach Lake, Glenn turned left onto a side road and pulled to a stop.

Music was blasting from the car radio. The girls made a pass at conversation, but their voices could barely be heard above the music. Glenn tried negotiating a U-turn to return to the highway. Suddenly the car plunged nose-first into a ditch.

"If I get stuck, it will be the first time," Glenn boasted.

He shifted the car into reverse and tried to back out of the ditch. But the wheels just spun, kicking up dirt and taking the car nowhere. On a second try, he gunned the motor and the car surged clear. Glenn turned the car around, and they all just sat there for a minute—catching their breaths.

Lorraine was shaken. She leaned forward and said: "Hey, Kristen, just for the hell of it, why don't you put your seat belt on?" But Kristen apparently could not hear her because of the blaring radio.

Then Lorraine, fearing that Glenn's drinking had made him incapable of driving safely, said: "Hey, Glenn, I'm fine. Why don't you let me drive?"

Glenn, directly in front of Lorraine, heard her. He looked at her, laughed, and replied: "Nobody drives my car."

He then returned to Highway 652 and drove into another ditch. This time, after extricating the car, Glenn headed west on the highway—back toward Honesdale. He was again racing along, passing other automobiles.

Now, directly ahead of him was a car carrying Michael Madan and Stacy Scheuren. Unable to spot their friends at

Kuester's, they were riding to a Honesdale bar where they hoped to find them.

It was 11:25 P.M. Michael Madan had just passed the G and L Body Shop on his right. Just ahead of him on the right was a dairy farm set down in a hollow. On the left, off in the distance, was a stand of pine and hemlock trees.

Rounding a curve in a no-passing zone marked with two solid yellow lines, Michael saw a flash of red whiz by on his left. Glenn Evans was passing him not only on a curve in a no-passing zone but also with a hill directly ahead.

"What an asshole!" Michael said.

"Yeah," Stacy replied.

Glenn swung to the right in front of Michael's car but did not pull entirely into the right lane. His left wheels were still well across the center lines. Glenn leaned over to kiss Kristen.

"Glenn!" Kristen screamed. "Glenn, watch it!"

Headlights had just popped over the crest of the hill straight ahead of them—the headlights of a Dodge Dart station wagon in which V. A. Conrad was taking his daughter home from their ice-cream run. Glenn's car swerved to the right. He mashed his brake pedal to the floor. The Duster screeched into a skid, swinging wildly to the left.

Glenn fought the skid. He struggled frantically with the steering wheel, trying to regain control. But the car continued sweeping to the left. It was no use. Glenn gave up—letting the car go where it would. The Duster fishtailed across the road, its right side facing the approaching Conrad station wagon.

The wagon slammed into the side of the Duster with a deafening boom. Both vehicles were twisted by the impact into grotesque hulks, as if some mad metal sculptor had pounded them into bewildering works of purported abstract art.

Michael Madan stopped and parked in the eastbound lane, his lights and flashers turned on to alert approaching drivers to the collision. Stacy Scheuren stood in the westbound lane, flagging down traffic. Michael went to see if he could help anyone hurt in the wreck. A passerby put in a call to the Honesdale barracks of the Pennsylvania State Police.

Minutes later, with sirens blaring and red lights flashing, state troopers Michael O'Day and William Dean arrived. Then came ambulances and rescue workers not only from Honesdale and Beach Lake but also from more distant towns such as Narrowsburg in New York and Hawley and White Mills in Pennsylvania.

Some occupants of the Duster and the station wagon were trapped inside the wreckage. It took rescue workers almost an hour—using a tool known as the Jaws of Life—to pry everyone from the mass of crushed steel.

Glenn Evans had staggered from his car and sprawled on the pavement, screaming that his leg hurt. V. A. Conrad was badly injured, but his daughter was worse. She would lose a leg as a result of the crash. Lorraine Cush had struck her head on the front seat at the moment of impact and could remember nothing of what had happened immediately afterward. Heidi Stacier also suffered memory loss. All she remembered of the accident was looking down after the collision and seeing nothing but blood and broken glass.

Kristen Umstadter had sustained the worst injuries—fractures of the ribs; punctures of the right lung; spinal fractures; a rupture of the right adrenal gland; and lacerations of the liver, kidneys, spleen, right hand, right shoulder, right foot, and left heel. Most seriously, the impact had severed her aorta.

Within minutes of the collision, Honesdale's golden girl—the town's voice against drunk driving—had bled to death on Route 652 in the wreckage of a car strewn with broken bottles and reeking of beer.

FOUR

Laraine and Dave Umstadter, waiting up for Kristen in the house on Erie Street, heard the sirens blowing for a long time, beginning about eleven-thirty. "There must have been a bad wreck," Laraine said idly.

It was not until midnight came and went without Kristen's arrival that Laraine and Dave showed any concern. Midnight was Kristen's curfew, and she never missed curfew. By twelve-twenty, when Kristen still had not arrived, Laraine was growing out-and-out worried.

She telephoned Lorraine Cush's home. No answer. That seemed strange. Honesdale was not the sort of town where telephones normally went unanswered after midnight. Next, Laraine called Heidi Stacier's home. A young boy answered, said Heidi had been hurt in an automobile accident and that most of the family had gone to see her at Wayne County Memorial Hospital. Laraine phoned the hospital but could get no information.

Now, trying to control their emotions but on the verge of panic, Laraine and Dave made the five-minute drive up Main Street to the hospital. They had barely entered the building when a nurse rushed up and asked: "Where have you been?"

"What do you mean, where have we been?" Laraine said. "Is our daughter here?"

The nurse did not answer. She led Laraine and Dave into a room where they could talk privately. "Is our daughter here?" Laraine asked more urgently.

"Yes," the nurse said. Laraine saw something in the nurse's eyes—an indefinable yet palpable signal.

"Is our daughter alive?" Laraine asked.

"No," the nurse said. "I'm sorry."

Laraine sagged against Dave. Both broke into tears. They were given a few minutes to try to compose themselves, then were taken to the hospital morgue to identify Kristen's body.

Dave would say later that neither he nor Laraine would ever be able to erase from their memories the sight of Kristen lying there on that hospital table. "I've seen that same thing in my mind a hundred—a million—times, I guess," he recalls. "I just kept thinking about her lying out there on that road, dying."

Travis Umstadter was out with friends when he heard there had been an accident and that Kristen had been taken to the hospital. But he did not immediately learn her condition. Travis drove to Wayne County Memorial, parked his car, and hurried toward the hospital entrance. Just before he reached the front door, he encountered his parents walking out to the parking lot. Travis took one look at his mother's face and knew instantly that Kristen was dead.

"No!" he shouted to the heavens. "No! No! No! No! No! No! No!"

Glenn Evans, Lorraine Cush, Heidi Stacier, and V. A. Conrad were all treated at Wayne County Memorial. But Kerstin Conrad, more seriously injured, was rushed in critical condition to the larger Community Medical Center in Scranton.

State troopers Michael O'Day and William Dean spent two hours at the accident scene—helping evacuate the victims, directing the clearing of the wreckage, and gathering physical evidence. Their investigation determined that Glenn Evans's Duster had left 216 feet of skid marks before colliding with Conrad's station wagon.

At about 1:15 A.M., the troopers arrived at Wayne County Memorial to question Glenn. They found him in a treatment room just off the emergency room. His clothing, they noted, was disheveled. His eyes were bloodshot. There was an odor of alcohol on his breath.

As they had been trained to do, the troopers followed a printed state police form in interviewing Glenn—asking a series of numbered questions on the form and filling in the appropriate responses. Block Eight on the questionnaire asked: "Have you been drinking?"

When O'Day asked him the question, Glenn replied: "Yes." He said he drank several beers during the round-trip to Scranton early in the evening, then drank some more at home, and was drinking from a bottle in the car shortly before the collision.

Immediately upon hearing Glenn's admission of drinking and driving, O'Day stopped him. "You have the right to remain silent," he said. "You have the right to have an attorney present. . . ." But Glenn agreed to continue the interrogation without benefit of counsel.

O'Day asked if he would consent to a test that would check the alcohol content of his blood.

"Yes," Glenn said.

A nurse drew a vial of blood from Glenn's arm. The vial was turned over to the troopers for later analysis by state police chemists.

Glenn did not yet know that Kristen was dead. He asked O'Day several times how Kristen was doing, but the trooper never answered. And, although Dave Umstadter entered the room at one point, O'Day instructed him to leave before he could talk to Glenn.

When O'Day asked Glenn to describe the events leading to the crash, Glenn told him: "We were on our way back home to Honesdale. I had been having trouble with the steering. I passed another car, and Kristen grabbed the steering wheel to try to steer the car. I guess she was scared by my driving. I got the steering wheel back, but I couldn't straighten the car out. I lost control and started to skid. I just let it go. I knew I was going to crash, so I just went with it."

Glenn had said nothing to his passengers about "having trouble with the steering," and a later check by state police safety experts would find nothing wrong with the Duster's steering mechanism. As for the contention that Kristen had grabbed the steering wheel just before the crash, it was a claim that Glenn would make repeatedly during the weeks to come.

But it was unprovable. Lorraine Cush said she had seen Kristen grab the wheel once earlier in the ride, but neither she nor Heidi Stacier had seen Kristen do so immediately before the crash. Moreover, there was no way of knowing whether Kristen might have helped cause the accident even if she had grabbed the wheel. By Glenn's account, Kristen had tried to steer the Duster away from the oncoming Dart. Whether turning the wheel to the right would have precipitated the skid that sent Glenn's car fishtailing across the road was unclear.

But Glenn nonetheless persisted in pressing that story. Later a warrant was drawn charging Glenn with homicide by motor vehicle while under the influence of alcohol, a lesser count of simple homicide by motor vehicle (not requiring proof of alcohol use), driving under the influence of alcohol, reckless driving, speeding, failing to stay on the right side of the road, and violation of various alcoholic-beverage laws.

He was taken into custody and driven to the Honesdale state police barracks to be photographed and fingerprinted. During the ride to the barracks, Glenn was seated in the front passenger seat of a police cruiser beside trooper O'Day. "Can I ask you a question?" Glenn said.

"Yes."

"What would you do if someone grabbed the steering wheel like this?" Glenn asked. He reached toward the wheel and simulated pulling it to the right.

"Who did that?" O'Day asked.

"That's what Kristen did."

"Why would she do that?"

"I was across the yellow line, and she got paranoid because she saw the lights coming."

"Why were you across the yellow line?"

"Only about a quarter of my car was over the line, and I had the car under control," Glenn said.

"How fast were you going?"

"I wasn't going fast at all."

The conversation ended there as the police cruiser pulled into the barracks parking lot. Glenn Evans would continue to tell that basic story. But it would not go undisputed. Nor would it necessarily help his case that the results of the blood test made at the hospital would show that his blood-alcohol level was .09, just below the .10 reading necessary under Pennsylvania law to establish intoxication. Since the blood test was taken two hours and ten minutes after the accident—giving Glenn a chance to sober up at least a bit—it would still be possible for prosecutors to try to prove through medical calculations that he had been legally drunk at the time of the crash. At his arraignment, Glenn pleaded not guilty to all the charges and was released on five thousand dollars' bail.

Word of Kristen Umstadter's death—and the circumstances under which it had occurred—struck Honesdale and Wayne County with the force of a thunderclap. The community had witnessed greater losses of life than had been inflicted by the wreck on Route 652. There had been multiple fatalities in automobile accidents, fires, and murders. But never in recent years had there been a calamity involving such a universally beloved figure as Kristen.

All that promise she had exhibited, all those hopes for her future, had been wiped out in an instant. And the cruelest blow, it seemed, was that this passionate crusader against drunk driving should herself be the victim of a highway crash in which the wreckage had been found drenched with beer.

Reactions to Kristen's death ranged from shock to sorrow to pragmatism. At radio station WDNH, on the morning after the accident, a technician searched through the collection of audio tapes regularly used on the air. He found the tape of Kristen telling listeners: "Friends don't let friends drive drunk." The technician immediately erased the tape, lest the voice of a dead Kristen Umstadter delivering a tragically inappropriate message be transmitted inadvertently over the airwaves.

At the Great Lakes naval base in Illinois, Allan Rutledge received an unexplained order to meet with a priest. When Allan appeared, he found the priest seated at a table—peering down at a collection of index cards. Allan identified himself. The priest shuffled through the cards, found the one he wanted,

and read the words, "Kristen Umstadter was killed in an automobile accident Friday night." The priest then stood and
walked from the room.

Allan went to his superiors and requested emergency leave to
return home. The leave was denied. He was told he could not
go home until he completed the eight weeks of basic training.

By Allan's description, he "just couldn't handle it." He had
been planning to wait until Christmas and then ask Kristen to
marry him. By Christmas she would have completed a semester
of college and both of them would have established better no-
tions of where their lives were headed. Actually, Laraine Umstadter says, Kristen would never have seriously entertained a
marriage proposal before completing college. But Allan did not
know that at the time.

Now Kristen was dead. A chaplain had coldly read Allan the
news from an index card. Allan's dream of a life with Kristen
was shattered, just like that. It was more than he could take.
He became bitter and rebellious.

Superiors gave him orders. He told them to stuff it. Other
recruits made remarks. He went after them, throwing wild
punches. What should have been eight weeks of basic training
stretched into twelve. In the end, Allan was discharged from
the Navy long before schedule. He never even made it to the
New London submarine base.

In Honesdale, the entire high school Class of '86—more than
two hundred graduates—filed somberly past Kristen's closed
coffin during brief funeral services at the Bryant Funeral Home.
Kristen's parents and brothers, pain etched in their very pores,
stared silently at the floor as her virtues, accomplishments, and
ambitions were enumerated.

Kristen was buried beneath the soil of the countryside she
loved near Lookout, in an old graveyard off a dirt and gravel
road behind the Lookout United Methodist Church. Her grave
lay near the back of the small cemetery, overseen by a stand of
towering evergreens. Nearby was a little farm, where pigs could
be heard snorting and shuffling around a barnyard. A modest
headstone would be erected over the grave—a marble monu-

ment bearing engravings of a dove with an olive branch at the upper right corner and a lamb at the lower left corner. The stone would be inscribed: KRISTEN MARIE UMSTADTER, 1967–1986. TO KNOW HER WAS TO LOVE HER.

But even before Kristen's burial, the Umstadters started raising questions about the circumstances of her death. No matter what Glenn Evans, Lorraine Cush, or Heidi Stacier said, the Umstadters contended that Kristen would never have willingly entered a car with a driver who was drinking. And, they argued, she certainly would never have carried beer into a car or swigged from an open bottle while driving.

Laraine Umstadter, in particular, maintained that Kristen must have been coaxed into Glenn's car. "She wouldn't even ride with Travis when he'd been drinking," Laraine says. "So I can't believe she would have ridden with Glenn Evans when he'd been drinking unless she was coaxed."

But there were other questions as well. The day after Kristen's death, Travis retrieved her Honda from the spot where she had left it in the parking lot outside Glenn's apartment. The car was unlocked. Kristen's family insisted she never left her car unlocked. Her car keys were in the Honda's ignition switch. Her family insisted she never left keys in her car. Her purse also was in the car. Her family insisted she never left her purse in the car. Moreover, there was no money in the purse when Travis found it. Kristen clearly had stopped at her bank and cashed her paycheck before going to Glenn's apartment on the night she died. Yet nobody could explain what had happened to the money.

If Kristen had been drunk on the night of her death, her condition might have provided answers to at least some of the open questions. But law-enforcement authorities, although insisting the precise results of a blood test performed on Kristen's body were confidential, did say that no evidence of intoxication had been found.

The remains of Glenn Evans's Plymouth Duster were towed after the crash to Burdick's Garage in Honesdale. Day after day, Travis drove to Burdick's and stood sobbing before the wreckage—staring into the mass of tangled metal as if searching for some hidden message. If there were actually any message, perhaps it lay in the broken beer bottles and the blood still visible in what was left of the car.

Each of the Umstadters mourned Kristen separately. Laraine visited Kristen's grave constantly, placing fresh flowers and mementos beside the headstone. Dave made visits on his own. Dave, Jr., refused to go to the cemetery or even talk about Kristen, remembering her in private. As for Travis, aside from staring at the wreckage of Glenn Evans's car, he drank. He drank even more than he had in the past—sometimes bursting into tears at the mention of Kristen's name.

Laraine Umstadter, beyond suffering the pain that could have been expected, nursed a variety of grievances. She was particularly disturbed that Glenn Evans had never visited or even called the Umstadter family to express regret over Kristen's death.

"If it had been Kristen who had survived, she would have gone to see her friend's parents," Laraine said more than once. "And, if she hadn't, I would have told her to go. I would have said, 'I'll go with you if you feel funny about it.'"

Glenn Evans's friends said he felt remorse over Kristen's death. But it was nonetheless true that he never made any attempt to express it to her family. Worse, he seemed entirely indifferent to the Umstadters' feelings. Word drifted back to them shortly after the accident that Glenn, far from showing contrition over Kristen's death, was complaining the accident had left him without a car. Then, when he bought another car several weeks later, he was seen driving as imprudently as he had in the past.

At various times, the Umstadters and their friends say, they saw Glenn speeding along local roads; passing other cars illegally; laughing; and, despite all, drinking beer. He also was seen performing so-called doughnuts—driving in circles, tipping his car so that two wheels lifted high off the ground—in a Honesdale parking lot. And, all the while, the Umstadters heard reports Glenn was boasting that he would beat the charges filed against him in Kristen's death.

Since Glenn could not afford to hire his own lawyer, responsibility for trying to help him beat those charges fell to the Wayne County public defender, Robert Bryan. In Wayne County, as in other sparsely populated Pennsylvania counties, not only the public defender but also the district attorney and his assistants serve just part-time while also conducting private law practices.

But Glenn was by no means shortchanged through the assignment of Bob Bryan to his case. Bryan, an informal man of medium build with a square jaw, brown hair, and penetrating brown eyes, was an aggressive advocate as both public defender and private counsel. He had been around the block, practicing law in Honesdale since 1973 and winning a reputation as a solid man to have in your corner.

"There are better lawyers than I am—not in this town but in the state of Pennsylvania," Bryan says. "I used to let that bother me when I lost a case. I thought some better lawyer might have won. But then I realized that I'm a good lawyer and, if I give it my best shot and lose, that's the way it is. I've had a lot more peace of mind since then."

There was, however, to be no peace of mind for Bryan in the Glenn Evans case. It was to become one of the most troubling episodes in his entire career.

Before taking on the case, Bryan heard stories describing Glenn as "a real dirtbag." But when Glenn became his client and came to his law office for several long interviews, Bryan recalls looking across the desk at him one day and thinking: This kid's not such a dirtbag, after all. I like this kid. He's a nice, quiet, polite kid. And he's still very much in love with Kristen Umstadter.

As often happens in such cases, sundry whispers about Kristen floated around town after her death. Some were patently ridiculous, others unprovable or unproved. Perhaps the most insidious to her family was a tale that Kristen—buckling under pressure from her parents to be perfect in every way—had once swallowed a handful of sleeping pills at a friend's party. "It never happened," Laraine Umstadter insists.

Still, the report persisted and found its way to Bob Bryan. When Bryan heard Glenn Evans's story about Kristen pulling the wheel just before the accident, he immediately associated that account with the rumored suicide attempt. He proposed trying to show at Glenn's trial that Kristen might have pulled the wheel in another attempt to take her life.

"No," Glenn told him. "I don't want to do that. I don't want to do anything to hurt Kristen's memory."

Glenn would not always be that circumspect about protecting Kristen's memory. But he would continue to insist that Bryan refrain from using the disputed—and perhaps spurious—sleeping-pill story. Bryan, fully prepared to use the story except for his client's objections, finally gave Glenn his way. "I work for my client," he explains. Nonetheless, after hearing Glenn's entire account, Bryan believed he could present a strong case at least against the most serious charge of homicide by motor vehicle while under the influence of alcohol.

The reading on Glenn's blood-alcohol test, Bryan concluded, did not support such a charge. Since the reading was slightly below the intoxication level, he did not see how any court would presume Glenn had been drunk at the time of the collision. To make a case of vehicular homicide while under the influence, the prosecution would be obliged to prove three points: that Glenn was driving the car, that he was under the influence of alcohol, and that the alcohol had rendered him incapable of safe driving. Bryan's best judgment was that the prosecution could prove Glenn was driving the car, but not the other two elements.

He questioned Glenn closely about accounts by other witnesses, who said he was driving seventy-five to eighty-five miles an hour and was well over the highway's double yellow lines just before the crash. Glenn told him emphatically: "I was going over fifty-five, but not seventy-five. Maybe sixty-five. I admit I was a little over the line, but Kristen grabbed the wheel."

"Well, you were speeding and you were driving recklessly,"

Bryan told him. "You passed another car over the double yellow lines. That was reckless driving. But that didn't cause the accident."

The Spartan room where Bob Bryan and Glenn Evans sat talking before a bare fireplace that day lay in the heart of Honesdale's legal community. From that room, in an old frame house converted to office space on downtown Court Street, Bryan could walk to the Wayne County Courthouse in less than a minute.

Most of the local law offices were headquartered in other converted homes around the rim of Honesdale's Central Park —a two-block island of greenery set directly before the courthouse. The park's centerpiece was a statue of a Union Army soldier, erected to commemorate Wayne County's Civil War dead "who fell that government of the people, by the people, and for the people shall not perish from the earth."

Bob Bryan could look past the monument and see, on the far side of the park, the private law office of his frequent courtroom combatant, District Attorney Ray Hamill. Shuttling constantly between that office and the DA's office in the courthouse, Hamill scrupulously conducted the public's business on public property and his private law practice on private property. A few doors down the street from Bryan's office was the law office of Hamill's chief assistant, Mark Zimmer, who had been assigned to prosecute Glenn Evans.

On Ninth Street, just off the park, stood the office of Lee Krause, an attorney retained by the Umstadter family to sue Glenn and anyone else who might be held liable in Kristen's death. And just up the street was the law office of John J. Koehler, where Laraine Umstadter worked as a legal secretary and paralegal.

The occupants of these law offices all knew each other well. Their professional paths crossed all the time—in their offices, in the courtroom, at the clerk's office at the courthouse (known in Pennsylvania as the prothonotary's office). The lawyers met regularly over lunch, as did the secretaries.

It was this tight little legal community, in a sense, that would be responsible for determining what was to become of Glenn Evans. But in a greater sense, that decision would belong not merely to the legal community but also to the broader community at large. And it would serve, in a curiously illuminating way, as a test of community character—a measure of what sort of town Honesdale really was.

FIVE

Any outlander trying to get a handle on the distinct local flavor of Honesdale, Pennsylvania, could do worse than to contemplate a conversation overheard one morning at that favorite Main Street hangout, the Towne House Diner, where Kristen Umstadter had once waited on tables.

It was shortly after seven o'clock. Two local cement-truck drivers plodded through the diner's front door in their high-topped work boots, eased down on stools at the left side of the counter, ordered ham and eggs, then sipped tentatively at the steaming cups of coffee the waitress placed before them without being asked. Both of them were in their forties, husky, with the weathered skin of men accustomed to the outdoors. The one called Dick was a six-footer with reddish-brown hair, a prominent Adam's apple, and a nasal, whiny voice. His companion, Charlie, was shorter but more muscular, with black hair, high cheekbones, and an air of you-bet-your-ass bravado.

On the counter before them stood a circular plastic dispenser filled with glazed doughnuts. Against the wall behind the counter were a machine that dispensed carbonated drinks, shelves filled with clean glasses, an array of coffee pots, and a small selection of bottled liquors. On the walls hung sundry framed photographs of old locomotives and train stations—reminders of Honesdale's days as a railroading center. In the center of the rear wall facing Dick and Charlie was a set of swinging doors leading to the kitchen. Waitresses, their arms loaded with dishes, kicked the doors open and then nimbly slid through the narrow passage before the doors could slam shut on them.

Dick was saying that he wanted to drop by a turkey raffle

that night—an annual event sponsored by the volunteer fire department in Equinunk, north of Honesdale. "I can't find anybody to go with me," he said.

"I'm not goin'," Charlie told him.

"Harry'd go if you'd go."

"Then he's not goin'."

"Oh, yeah, you're for *paid* fire departments," Dick said.

"That's right."

"But volunteer fire departments spread more goodwill."

"I don't want to spread goodwill," Charlie said. "I'm against it."

"But what if you need a volunteer fire department to save your house?"

"I don't want volunteer firemen to save my house. I want 'em to let it burn. All they'd do is save one wall. Then the insurance adjuster would come out and say: 'We can't pay you a hundred percent on your house—just forty percent. See that wall; it didn't burn.' "

"What about if they're saving your life?"

"Hell, they'd probably run over somebody else with the fire engine and kill him on the way. Anyway, I'm surprised you'd want to go to a turkey raffle right now—during the deer season —since you don't like to hunt deer. Everybody's gonna be saying, 'Hi, Dick, did you get your deer, did you get your deer?' What are you gonna tell 'em—that you don't like to hunt deer?"

"That's true," Dick said.

"Do you like the smell of Limburger cheese?" Charlie asked him.

"No."

"Well, you know, those deer hunters are always smearing themselves with Limburger cheese so the deer can't pick up the human smell on 'em. They're gonna get right in your face at the turkey raffle, with that Limburger smell, and ask: 'Did you get your deer? Did you get your deer?' "

"Maybe I won't go to the turkey raffle."

"That Limburger's gonna smell real rank."

"I'm not goin'," Dick said, throwing up his hands.

All of this is not, by any means, to say that Honesdale is a hick town. It may lie out in the countryside, but it is far from some sleepy backwater. Quite the contrary—it is a lively, sophisticated little town with a rich, colorful history.

Honesdale was once the world's largest coal-storage center. It also was the site of the first railroad run made by a steam locomotive in the United States. And it was in Honesdale—in a small building still standing among the law offices on Ninth Street—that Horace Greeley met in 1859 with Republican leaders to plan the strategy leading to Abraham Lincoln's nomination and election as president the following year.

Lyman Lemnitzer was born in Honesdale on August 29, 1899, son of a local shoe-company executive. He would become a World War II army hero—closely escaping death on several secret missions—and later would serve as commander of United Nations forces in the Korean War, chairman of the Joint Chiefs of Staff, and supreme commander of NATO.

An earlier military man from Honesdale, General Edgar Jadwin, led one of the first American regiments to enter the fighting in France during World War I. Jadwin, an engineer, also served as General George Goethals's chief aide in the construction of the Panama Canal and as commander of the Army Corps of Engineers.

On Honesdale's Willow Avenue, adjacent to what is now Lincoln Elementary School, a historical marker stands beside a bumpy, rock-strewn ball field. The marker attests that in 1898 and 1899 Christy Mathewson—later to become one of the premier pitchers in major-league history—was virtually unhittable as the star of the Honesdale Eagles.

Also leaving marks well beyond the confines of Wayne County were such Honesdale natives as Art Wall, Jr., named professional golfer of the year in 1959 and renowned as the world's hole-in-one champion (he made forty-one of them in twenty-two years); Ruth McGinnis, the world women's pocket-billiards champion in the 1930s (she also defeated many of the top men's players—competing in 1,532 matches, mostly against men, and losing only twenty-nine from 1933 to 1938); and songwriter Dick Smith ("Winter Wonderland," "When a Gypsy Makes His Violin Cry," "It Looks Like an Early Fall").

As elsewhere, geography has been an important force in determining the course of Honesdale's development. The town is perched high in the Poconos, almost a thousand feet above sea level. From the west, the Lackawaxen River flows through the heart of town, merges with the Dyberry River, and turns south. To the east, the more imposing Delaware River serves as the border between Pennsylvania and New York.

The first known inhabitants of the Honesdale area were members of the Lenni Lenape Indian tribe, who originally settled along the Delaware River and then moved west. By the time the Pennsylvania legislature established Wayne County in 1798, white settlers had begun arriving. Many were New Englanders who had fought in the Revolution.

Coal served as the primary impetus for Honesdale's development. Rich anthracite deposits were found in 1814 near Carbondale, eighteen miles west of Honesdale. By the 1820s, coal was being hauled by mule to Honesdale, then shipped along a canal to the Hudson River en route to New York City. Coal and the canal brought settlers, work, and capital to Honesdale —named for Philip Hone, a future New York City mayor (1826 to 1827) and head of the company that ran the canal.

As an efficiency measure, the canal company explored using steam locomotives to haul the coal from Carbondale to Honesdale. A steam locomotive called the *Stourbridge Lion* was bought in England and shipped to Honesdale, where tracks were laid for a test run. On August 8, 1829, the *Stourbridge Lion* made a successful three-mile run—the first steam-locomotive trip to take place in this country. It was eventually decided, however, that locomotives would be too heavy for the tracks then available for transporting the coal. The *Stourbridge Lion* wound up in the Smithsonian Institution. But an ingenious gravity railroad was later devised for delivering the coal—using a series of stationary engines to pull trains to hilltops, then release them to coast downhill.

Honesdale was incorporated in 1831 as a borough of Wayne County, a status it retains today. Early ordinances passed by the borough council banned horse racing and puppet shows. Borough fathers were not about to let Honesdale degenerate into some wild boom town.

During its early years the town was choked with coal awaiting shipment to New York. At one point, 575,000 tons of coal were heaped on the Honesdale docks—the largest coal pile in the world. But conventional railroads eventually replaced the canal and the gravity railroad. New routes were found for shipping coal to market. By 1899 the gravity railroad had made its last run. By 1919 there was nothing left of the Honesdale coal pile.

Railroading and local manufacturing enterprises took up some of the slack in the local economy. For a time, Honesdale and Wayne County became centers of the shoemaking and cut-glass industries. Today, though, only remnants of those industries continue to operate, along with factories producing underwear, sleepwear, and women's blouses. Dairy farming, just as it has for years, remains a leading local occupation. Many farms have been owned by the same families for more than a century. But the town's biggest employer, Moore Business Forms, did not arrive until 1964—lured by a community industrial-development group.

Honesdale's population had reached 5,662 by 1950. In later years, however, the town suffered new economic setbacks. Factories closed, railroads cut back operations, some residents were drawn to bigger towns. Today the population is estimated at fifty-one hundred.

But surrounding Wayne County is experiencing substantial growth—a 14-percent population increase since 1980. Many new residents are attracted by the county's recreational advantages, among them 112 lakes. Recreation, in fact, is now one of the county's leading sources of income. There are more than forty summer camps and numerous fishing, boating, hunting, and skiing facilities.

Day-to-day life in Honesdale today seems not much at variance from life in countless small towns across America—kids riding off to school in their yellow buses, adults cruising off to work in their four-wheel-drives, families saying grace over dinner tables. Honesdale is the sort of town where local custom dictates that a driver will come to a dead stop to permit a pedestrian to cross Main Street.

Among the town's more venerable structures is Wayne County Courthouse, where Glenn Evans would stand trial in Kristen Umstadter's death and where accused criminals had been brought before the bench for more than a hundred years. The courthouse is not truly a handsome building, but it offers a certain timeless charm—a three-story, red-brick edifice with white columns framing its main entrance and with a modest cupola above.

It also offers a controversial history, including an unsuccessful attempt to impeach the county's presiding judge for ordering construction of the building in the face of an 1877 taxpayer vote rejecting the project. For years after the building opened in 1880, the county was divided into bitterly antagonistic anti-courthouse and procourthouse forces. A century later, similar controversy erupted when a modern annex was added to the original courthouse.

Somehow it seemed fitting that the Glenn Evans case would be set for trial in a courthouse with that sort of troubled history, for the Evans case and the events flowing from it were destined to bring nothing but trouble descending on Honesdale —trouble such as the town had never seen.

SIX

While Glenn Evans awaited trial in Honesdale, Travis Umstadter found himself sprawled one sultry summer night across the bed of a motel room in Smithfield, North Carolina. He was alone. He was depressed. He was miserable. He could not come to terms with the loss of his sister.

Travis was in North Carolina at that particular moment not by design but by a quirk of timing. Before Kristen's death, he had signed up for an eight-week course—learning to drive tractor-trailers—at a commercial truck-driving school in Smithfield. When Kristen was killed, he considered postponing the trip but eventually decided it was important for him to get on with his life. A week and a half after Kristen's funeral, Travis was on his way to North Carolina.

Now, though, he found himself not only despondent but also desperately lonely. He missed Kristen. He missed his parents. And he missed his girlfriend, a pretty social worker named Chrissy Striffler who lived not far from the new home the Umstadters were building. Travis and Chrissy had been dating for months, and the romance was getting serious. Chrissy, a transplant from New Jersey, was tall, slender, and brown-haired. Her approach to life—earnest, purposeful—conveniently balanced Travis's determination to take it one day at a time. Chrissy seemed devoted to her work at a job center across the state line from Honesdale in Callicoon, New York. She also seemed devoted to Travis, a circumstance that made his separation from her all the harder.

The other students at the truck-driving school were all strangers to Travis. He made no attempt to form friendships or tell anyone his problems. Instead, in the solitude of his motel room, he brooded over his loneliness and Kristen's death.

Immediately after Kristen was killed, Travis had stopped drinking because, in his words, "I thought I owed it to myself." But the cessation had lasted only a week. Now, succumbing to old habits, Travis went looking for a palliative that might help him forget his troubles.

A half-mile down the road there was a small convenience store. It did not, of course, stock regional Yankee beers such as Genessee. But it did have plenty of Bud and Miller. Travis loaded up on six-packs and carried them back to his motel room.

There, still alone, he sloshed down one can, then another, then another and another. He did not stop until he was so thoroughly drunk that there was nothing to do but collapse into sleep.

The routine became familiar over the two months Travis spent in North Carolina. Every other night or so, he would make the trip to the convenience store and then drink until he dropped.

When he returned to Honesdale, Travis recognized that he had merely been postponing the inevitable during all those weeks in North Carolina. "I was confronted with a problem that I realized I was running from," he would later recall. "And there was no more running. I had to deal with reality now as it was."

The reality was that he and his family were still tormented by all those questions about Kristen's death. How had she come to be in Glenn Evans's car when Glenn was drinking? Had she been coaxed into the car? And all the rest—the questions about why Kristen's car had been left unlocked, why she had not taken her purse with her on the fatal ride, what had happened to the money from her paycheck.

Every evening, with an oil painting of Kristen staring eerily down at them from a wall, the Umstadters would sit at their kitchen table and endlessly rehash the minute details of what they knew about her death. Laraine would press Travis to seek answers to their questions. He, better than his parents, knew the young people who might be able to provide information. He was out and around town.

"What do you hear?" Laraine would ask Travis each evening.

"Nothing," he would reply in frustration.

But if the Umstadters were not finding answers to their questions, they *were* accumulating information about Glenn Evans —information that enraged them. Stories came back to them asserting that Glenn had been heard laughing about Kristen's death. One story contended that Glenn, still claiming Kristen had pulled the steering wheel, had told friends: "The bitch got what she deserved."

That was more than Dave Umstadter could take. He telephoned District Attorney Ray Hamill at home. "What can be done about this?" he asked. "This is too much to bear." Dave said he wanted to phone Glenn and tell him off.

But Hamill urged him not to make the call—to talk instead to Mark Zimmer, the assistant DA prosecuting the Evans case. "You could blow our case if you talk to Glenn," Hamill said. Dave agreed to refrain from communicating with Glenn in any way.

Still, it soon became clear that a seething antagonism was building between Kristen Umstadter's survivors and their friends, on one side, and Glenn Evans, his relatives, and friends on the other. The Umstadter camp was livid at the thought that Glenn, although responsible for taking Kristen's life, might well get off with a short prison sentence or no punishment at all. There were angry confrontations and threats between the two camps.

Kristen's former boyfriend, Allan Rutledge, encountered Glenn's brother Mark one night at a party. "Glenn's a dead man," Allan told him. Words were exchanged, but the two of them did not come to blows. (Allan was a head taller and a good forty pounds heavier than Mark.) Travis expressed his own hatred toward Glenn both publicly and privately.

One day, Glenn was standing in the office of a Texaco station on Main Street with the station's owner, Elwin Ostrander. They looked out the window and saw Travis stop his car in the street, blocking traffic outside the station. Chrissy Striffler was seated beside him. Travis ignored the cars lining up behind his Pontiac. He reached across Chrissy—his face contorted with rage—and expressed his contempt for Glenn by defiantly thrusting his right middle index finger skyward.

In private, Travis called Glenn an asshole and told friends: "He should pay for what he did." More than a few responded that it was unfair for Kristen to be dead and Glenn alive.

Day by day, week by week, the bitterness intensified as Glenn's case remained unresolved. Even the arrival of the Christmas season brought no alleviation. For the Umstadters, the holiday atmosphere merely seemed to emphasize their loss. Kristen had always been the one in their family who most enjoyed Christmas. Without her, what was there to celebrate?

"Don't put up a Christmas tree," Travis urged Laraine. "The tree was always for Kristen."

Laraine gave him his way. Then, on Christmas Eve, Travis changed his mind. He asked Laraine to put up a tree after all. She again obliged him—scrambling around to get the decorations hung in time. But by Christmas Day Travis could not stand the tree's sight. It reminded him constantly that Kristen was gone. By nightfall, so was the tree.

As for Glenn Evans, he did not pass a joyous Christmas, either. The prospect of his trial loomed ominously before him and, despite his talk of beating the charges, he was fully aware that his next Christmas might well be spent behind bars.

Defense attorney Bob Bryan, trying to prevent that, proposed a plea bargain immediately after the turn of the year. He offered to plead Glenn guilty if the DA's office would drop its most serious charges—those accusing Glenn of homicide by motor vehicle. Word of the proposed plea bargain brought an explosion of protest from the Umstadters. Dave Umstadter, incredulous at the mere suggestion of such a deal, wrote an angry letter published in a local newspaper, the *Wayne Independent:*

My daughter, Kristen, lost her life on August 16, 1986, in an auto accident. The driver of the car (a minor), by his own admission, was speeding excessively. My daughter will be dead forever, and I can spend the rest of my life wondering what her life might have been like had she lived.

Her death was the result of the careless and irresponsible acts of the driver. There is now plea bargaining going on to get him a lighter sentence. This is the way our judicial system works.

The driver has been charged with nine counts, among them reckless driving, homicide by vehicle, homicide by vehicle while under the influence of alcohol and involuntary manslaughter. Why should any of these counts be bargained with? Considering my daughter's sentence and the fact that we, her family, must face the rest of our lives without her, why shouldn't this driver face all counts as charged and be sentenced accordingly?

I wonder how some of the people who work in this system would feel about plea bargaining if they had to visit their son or daughter at the cemetery.

In the end, the district attorney's office rejected the proposed plea bargain. On January 19, 1987, five months after Kristen's death, Glenn Evans went on trial. Laraine, Dave, and Travis Umstadter were all in the courtroom. Perhaps, they had told each other repeatedly in advance of the trial, some of their questions would be answered from the witness stand.

Juries for criminal trials are chosen in a magnificent old

courtroom in the original section of Wayne County Courthouse. It is a spacious chamber offering an abundance of room for large jury panels. Hanging on the wall behind the judge's bench, as if overseeing the proceedings, is an enormous carving of an eagle—its wingspan reaching more than eight feet across the front of the room. The ceiling is forty feet high. There are marble fireplaces, no longer used, on each side of the courtroom. The judge's bench, the witness and jury boxes, the counsel tables, and the clerk's desk are all crafted from handsome dark woods. At the rear there are twenty-four rows of spectator benches.

Since Pennsylvania calls itself a commonwealth, the prosecution side in a criminal case is known not as the State but the Commonwealth. In the case styled *Commonwealth of Pennsylvania* v. *Glenn Evans,* the Commonwealth was embodied by Chief Assistant District Attorney Mark Zimmer—an intense young Honesdale native and Duquesne University alumnus with sharp features, a firm jaw, and a sober countenance. Zimmer and Bob Bryan, representing Glenn, painstakingly picked a jury that Monday morning.

Because of the press of other court business, the case was then adjourned until the following afternoon. When it resumed, the trial proper would take place in a newer, smaller courtroom on the fourth floor of the courthouse annex—modern, austere, providing better acoustics than the old courtroom but infinitely less character.

Presiding over the trial was Judge Robert Conway of the Pennsylvania Court of Common Pleas. A graduate of the University of Scranton and Brooklyn Law School, Conway had been the Wayne County district attorney before his election to the bench in 1979. He was forty-eight, a stocky, jowly man with black hair, a round face, and a double chin. On the bench, along with his black judicial robe, Conway often wore a dour expression.

It was even more dour than usual when the Evans trial reconvened on January 20, for Bob Bryan disclosed that after putting the court through the entire jury-selection process, he and Glenn had decided to waive a jury trial. They would take their chances on a verdict rendered by Judge Conway alone. Under the law, the Commonwealth could not object to Bryan's motion for a nonjury trial. Bryan was not obliged to specify any reasons for the motion, and he did not. But what had happened was that Bryan had changed his mind overnight—not because he had any objections to the particular jury chosen but because his strategy had changed.

Initially the strategy had called for putting the case before a jury. Since a jury verdict would have to be unanimous, Bryan hoped to swing at least one juror to Glenn's side and gain no worse than a hung jury. But after the jury had been picked, Bryan decided that this case was more likely to be decided on nuances of law than strictly on the facts. He felt Judge Conway would have a firmer grasp than a jury of those nuances. Thus, after discussing all the options at length with Glenn, Bryan chose the nonjury trial.

Conway was less than ecstatic over the waste of court time inherent in picking a jury that would never serve. "It would have been nice if we had talked about this prior to yesterday," he told Bryan testily.

"I am aware of that," Bryan said.

Nonetheless, the judge granted the motion for a nonjury trial. The opposing lawyers dispensed with the opening statements they would have delivered to a jury. Testimony began immediately.

Zimmer called as his first witness Stacy Scheuren, the young teacher who had been riding in the car Glenn passed just before the fatal collision. "Do you remember the night of August the fifteenth, 1986?" Zimmer asked her.

"Yes, I do," she said. "I went out to celebrate because I had just received notice that I had gotten a job at Narrowsburg to teach."

Scheuren told of going to Kuester's lounge in Beach Lake with her boyfriend, Michael Madan, and then riding with him down Route 652 toward another bar called the Wagon Wheel. They had looked in vain for friends at Kuester's, she said.

"What, if anything, do you recall happening as you were riding toward Honesdale on Route 652 that evening?" Zimmer asked.

"We were going right by the G and L Body Shop when all of a sudden a car flashed by us," Scheuren testified. "It was going very fast. My boyfriend swore at them. He couldn't believe that they were going so fast. Then I looked at the speedometer and we were going about fifty-five, so they were going much faster than we were."

"Could you tell us what were the center-line markings in the road at the point where the car went by?"

"Double yellow."

"Was the road straight?"

"No. It was curved and it was just coming over the crest of a hill."

Scheuren said she lost sight of the other car momentarily as it sped over the hill, but that she then picked it up again. "The car had just made it over safely to the right side of the road, made it over just fine," she testified. "And then it hit the edge of the road, the curve, and it seemed to overcompensate. It turned almost a one-eighty-degree and hit the oncoming car that was coming up."

Q. You say it turned one-eighty-degree. Did it go across the road?

A. Yes, after it hit the curve, it spun around and came into the other car. The passenger side hit the oncoming car.

Q. In which lane did the collision occur?

A. The oncoming car's lane.

Q. After the accident, what did you do?

A. I got out of the car and Mike did also. The boy that was driving the car that passed us, he got out of the car and immediately stated that "she" had touched the wheel. He had swerved and "she touched the fuckin' wheel." And, after that, I was trying to stop traffic.

On cross-examination, Bob Bryan asked Scheuren whether she was alarmed to see Glenn's car swerve over to the right edge of the road. "Was it so radical or sharp that it startled you?"

"I was concerned, yes," she replied. "I will have to say that I was very concerned at that speed going at the edge of the road."

Michael Madan, a student at Franklin and Marshall College in Lancaster, Pennsylvania, testified that "a red flash" had whizzed by his car. As Glenn's Duster passed over the hill, he said, he could see the beams of headlights coming in his direction.

"I had an apprehensive feeling," Madan testified. "I was watching the headlights coming and, after a couple of seconds or so, I saw the moment of impact."

When he stopped his car with his lights on the wreckage, he noticed that the Duster's driver had already gotten out of the car. Mark Zimmer, pointing at Glenn Evans, asked: "That driver, would that be the individual on the right here?"

"Yes," Madan replied. He said he saw a girl in the wreckage and asked Glenn: "Is she all right?"

"No, she ain't all right," Glenn answered. "She fucked with the wheel, man. She fucked with the wheel."

Bob Bryan asked Madan on cross-examination whether Glenn's car, although traveling at high speed, appeared stable when it passed him. Madan said that it did.

"Then the car cut back in?" Bryan asked.

"I never saw the car cut back into my lane cleanly," Madan replied. "At that point I looked at the oncoming car and the headlights."

"Do you remember the road condition, sir?"

"Yes, it was dry."

V. A. Conrad, the driver of the station wagon involved in the collision, testified only briefly—saying he could not remember the crash in detail because of the shock he had suffered. "But I did have a flashback of parts of the accident," he said. "There was a car that came over the hill at high speed. He was still on his side of the road at that point, and then the car turned sideways on the road with the front end of it on my side and the back end on his side. And that is where my memory goes, a split second before impact."

"Do you remember if you were in your lane?" Zimmer asked.

"Yes, I was."

"Did you receive any injuries as a result of this accident?"

Bob Bryan was on his feet. "I would object," he said. "It is not relevant. It might be for civil trials, certainly, but not for a criminal—"

Zimmer argued that it *was* relevant, merely to show the force of the impact. Judge Conway ruled that Conrad could say whether he was injured but could not describe the injuries. "Did you receive injuries?" the judge asked.

"I did receive injuries," Conrad said.

"That question only," the judge ordered. The ruling effectively barred Conrad not only from describing his own injuries but also from revealing that his eleven-year-old daughter had lost a leg as a result of the collision.

State trooper Michael O'Day told of rushing to the accident scene with trooper William Dean minutes after the crash was reported to the police dispatcher. O'Day said he and Dean helped the injured and directed traffic, then began gathering and photographing physical evidence. He described examining the skid marks left by Glenn Evans's car on its path to the collision.

"How long were those skid marks, if you measured them?" Zimmer asked.

"They were paced off at two hundred sixteen feet," O'Day testified. He said the impact of the crash sent the frames of both cars collapsing onto the pavement.

The trooper then told of going to the hospital and questioning Glenn. He said he asked Glenn whether he had been drinking and recorded the response verbatim in his handwritten notes: "The subject replied, 'Yes,' and he stated that he had been drinking at home and he had further stated that he had been drinking from an open container prior to the collision." O'Day said he then read Glenn his rights, but Glenn continued telling him about the accident—making the claims that he had been having trouble with the car's steering and that Kristen had pulled the wheel to the right.

Upon request, O'Day said, Glenn agreed to take a test to check the alcohol content of his blood. Blood was drawn for the test at 1:35 A.M. Zimmer and Bryan agreed to stipulate the test showed that Glenn's blood-alcohol content at 1:35, more than two hours after the accident, was .09 percent—just below the .10 level required to prove intoxication.

Four days after the collision, O'Day went to the garage where Glenn's car had been towed and shot additional pictures of the wreckage. "There were two Michelob bottles, covered with blood and broken, and a cardboard six-pack carrier covered with blood found in the Evans vehicle in the area between the front seats," he testified. "They were jammed down between the seats."

Bob Bryan, on cross-examination, tried to establish that there was no conclusive evidence from Glenn's appearance and demeanor after the accident that he was drunk. O'Day testified that Glenn smelled of alcohol, his clothing was disheveled, and his eyes were bloodshot.

"Officer, you testified as to the bloodshot eyes," Bryan said. "Were you telling the court that the bloodshot eyes are a sign that, if present, indicates the use of alcohol? Or are you telling the court that can be one of the signs of use of alcohol?"

"It is one of the signs," O'Day said.

Q. You spoke with the subject, did you not, sir?

A. Yes, I did.

Q. He spoke normally at the time, did he not?

A. Normally, yes. Slow, but nothing, you know, it was a quiet speak.

Q. No slurring in his speech?

A. No, there was no slurring.

Prosecutor Zimmer, trying to prove Glenn was legally drunk at the time of the accident even if his blood-alcohol content later tested below the intoxication level, called an expert witness to the stand. Dr. Young W. Lee, a Chinese émigré, was both a pathologist at Wayne County Memorial Hospital and the elected county coroner.

Zimmer asked Lee a long hypothetical question based on circumstances identical to those in the Evans case—including a twenty-year-old driver with a .09 blood-alcohol reading two hours and ten minutes after an accident. "Doctor, based upon that hypothetical situation, can you, within a reasonable degree of medical certainty, render an opinion as to whether the blood-alcohol content of the driver at the time of the accident would have been higher than point zero nine percent, lower than point zero nine percent, or the same?"

Lee answered without hesitation. "I think alcohol was absorbing directly from the stomach as well as the small intestine," he said. "So alcohol level was reaching the peak about half an hour to one and a half hour [after the alcohol was swallowed]. An accident occurred possibly at time of peak. I think the time of the accident alcohol level is higher than after actual withdrawing of blood two hours later."

Under cross-examination, Lee conceded that he could not say exactly when the driver's blood-alcohol level would have reached its peak. "But there is the medically proved theory, thirty minutes to ninety minutes," he said.

For Laraine, Dave, and Travis Umstadter—no matter how zealous the search for answers to their questions about Kristen's death—hearing the testimony of each witness at the trial was in some way painful. But the testimony of the remaining witnesses would stretch beyond the painful to the absolutely excruciating and, from the Umstadters' perspective at least, the occasionally infuriating.

Called as the next witness was one of Kristen's companions on the night of the fatal collision, Heidi Stacier. Heidi was still only sixteen and an eleventh-grader.

"Heidi, do you remember the night of August fifteenth, 1986?" Zimmer asked. "Do you remember what you did that night?"

"I went out with Kristen Umstadter," Heidi replied.

"And nobody else?"

"Lorraine Cush."

Heidi told of Kristen picking her up at her home, of riding to the bank so Kristen could cash her paycheck, of meeting Lorraine at the Umstadter home, and then going to Kuester's.

"Why did you go to Kuester's?" Zimmer asked.

"To get beer."

"Whose idea was it to get beer?"

"Everyone's."

"What is Kuester's?"

"It is a bar."

"When you got out to Kuester's, what happened?"

"Kristen went in to Kuester's."

"Anybody else go in?"

"No."

"Did she come back out?"

"Yes, after about five minutes."

"What, if anything, did she have with her when she came out?"

"She had two six-packs of Michelob beer."

Heidi testified the girls then rode around Honesdale, drinking the beer. She said they finished one six-pack, with each of the girls drinking two beers. Then they rode to Glenn Evans's apartment. Heidi said they found Glenn sitting on a couch and talking to his friend Mark Ordnung. Loud music was resounding through the apartment.

Q. Whose idea was it to go to Glenn's?
A. Kristen's.
Q. Do you know why she wanted to go up there?
A. Because she liked him.
Q. How did the defendant react to seeing you there?

Q. He acted as if he didn't want us there. He acted like he was drunk.

Q. What did his eyes look like?

A. They were bloodshot.

Q. What did his hair look like?

A. A mess.

Q. What about his clothes?

A. A mess.

Q. What did you do at the defendant's house?

A. We talked and listened to music and played darts.

Q. Where was the defendant during this time?

A. Outside talking to Kristen.

Heidi testified Kristen stayed outside with Glenn for about twenty minutes, then returned to the apartment and told her: "Glenn is acting like a jerk." By that time, Heidi said, she was getting bored and told Kristen she wanted to leave. Everyone went outside, and Mark Ordnung drove off in his own car. Heidi said Kristen then announced: "We're going for a ride in Glenn's car."

Mark Zimmer asked: "Did it bother you to get into the defendant's car?"

Heidi replied: "I had second thoughts because I knew he was drinking and he had a reputation for driving bad."

"Objection!" Bob Bryan shouted.

"Sustained as to the last part, not the first part," Judge Conway ruled.

Despite her misgivings, Heidi said, she climbed into Glenn's Duster with the others. "Kristen was in the passenger seat, I was behind Kristen, and Lorraine was next to me," she said.

"Was there any beer in the car?" Zimmer asked.

"Yes."

"Who brought the beer in the car?"

"Glenn."

"Where did he put the beer?"

"On the console between the seats."

"Was there any open beer in the car?"

"Yes. In Glenn's lap."

Heidi then described the ride toward Beach Lake, getting stuck in a ditch, and hearing Glenn say: "If I get stuck, it will be the first time." She saw Lorraine leaning forward to talk to Glenn, but could not hear what was said because of the loud music blasting from the radio.

"What is the next thing that you remember after that?" Zimmer asked.

"Looking down at my legs and all I saw was glass and blood," Heidi said.

"Did you learn after that that you had been in an accident?"

"Yes."

"Were you injured in that accident?"

"Yes."

When Zimmer finished questioning Heidi, Bryan's cross-examination took her back over her story of Kristen buying the beer at Kuester's—a section of her testimony that would prove particularly hard for the Umstadter family to accept. ("I don't believe that!" Laraine Umstadter would later insist. "I'll never believe that as long as I live!")

Bryan asked Heidi: "Now, after everybody had the idea to get beer, you went up to Kuester's and got the beer?"

"Yes," Heidi said.

Q. Kristen went in?

A. Yes.

Q. She came out with two six-packs, is that right?

A. Yes.

Q. You testified that the three of you girls drove around and drank basically one six-pack, is that right?

A. Yes.

Q. When you got to Glenn's, did you have anything to drink in there?

A. No.

Q. Did anybody offer you anything to drink?

A. No.

Q. That is why you got bored?

A. No.

Q. Why did you get bored?

A. Conversation.

Q. Well, they were older kids than you, isn't that right? You turned sixteen a few months before?

A. Yes.

Q. Nobody else in the group was as young as you were?

A. No.

Lorraine Cush followed Heidi to the witness stand. She supported Heidi's account of the purchase of the beer—saying Kristen entered Kuester's alone, stayed about five minutes, and emerged with two six-packs of Michelob Light. She also testified, under Zimmer's questioning, that each of the girls drank two beers while riding around Honesdale in Kristen's car.

When they reached Glenn's apartment, Lorraine said, Kristen and Glenn sat together on a couch and talked. She said she and Heidi could not hear the conversation because of the loud music. "So we just sat there and presumed they were just, like, having a little bit of a spat because Kristen said she was worried about going up to Glenn's house because she had told Glenn that she wasn't going out that night."

"What was Glenn doing when you got there?" Zimmer asked.

"When we walked in, there was beer there. He was holding a beer."

Lorraine said Glenn carried a paper bag containing more beer when the girls left the apartment for the ride in his car. "Was there any open beer in the car?" Zimmer asked.

"Yes," Lorraine testified. "Glenn had one. Heidi and I were, like, splitting one. We each had, like, a sip of it."

"Where was the one that Glenn had, if you remember?"

"Between his legs."

"Anybody else have anything to drink?"

"I can't remember whether Kristen had one or not. I really don't think she did, though."

"Now, Lorraine, do you remember the defendant's manner of driving from the time he left his house that night?"

"Yes, I do. Maybe the term is reckless. From the time we left, his driving all night, it was—I don't know. It was dangerous. When we pulled out of his driveway onto Route Six, he spun the car and we kind of fishtailed onto Route Six. From there on, we drove very fast. When we took turns, we took them wide."

"Wide?" Zimmer asked. "You mean you were over the line?"

"Yes."

Lorraine described Glenn driving down Honesdale's Main Street, his left wheels across the center line, and another driver honking for him to move over. As they rode out Route 652, she said, Glenn continued "driving very fast, still taking turns wide and, once in a while, we would hit the right berm of the curve and the car would shake."

"Do you remember anything happening on the way out toward Beach Lake relative to Glenn's being near or over the yellow line?" Zimmer asked.

"I remember being over the yellow line and we were passing," Lorraine said. "There is a place—it's got a lot of machinery and stuff—and I remember a car coming toward us, and Kristen reached over and pulled us into the right lane to keep us from hitting a car."

A short time later, Lorraine testified, Glenn turned off on a side road and got stuck. It was then, she said, that she suggested he let her drive but Glenn replied that nobody else drove his car. As for the fatal accident itself, Lorraine's testimony added several details to Heidi's account. After Glenn passed Michael Madan's car, Lorraine said, he did not initially pull all the way into the right lane. "We kind of stayed with our left wheels over the yellow lines," she testified.

"How do you know that?" Zimmer asked.

"Because I saw Glenn leaning over to try to kiss Kristen. I could clearly see the road because he wasn't in the way."

"Then what happened as he was leaning over to try to kiss Kristen?"

"I saw two bright lights coming over like a ridge or around a turn and I remember hearing Kristen scream and the next thing I knew we jerked to the right and jerked to the left and we started to spin."

Lorraine's face was suddenly contorted in anguish. Tears formed in her eyes. She fought for control.

"Take it easy," Zimmer told her. "I know this isn't easy. After you jerked to the right, do you remember what the defendant did?"

Lorraine, after pausing to compose herself, replied: "He sat up and took the wheel and spun it around to the left and we started to spin counterclockwise to the left."

"What did you do then?"

"I remember after seeing the lights and starting to spin I just struck my head on the front seat, and I don't remember anything—"

Zimmer asked whether Lorraine had talked to Glenn since the night of the collision. She said she had, initially during a chance encounter when she returned from Duquesne University for the Christmas holiday. Lorraine said she happened upon Glenn while shopping at the Turkey Hill market in Honesdale. Glenn told her he was confused about what had happened the night of the accident. He asked if he could talk to her about it. When she agreed, he telephoned her the following morning and arranged for her to come to see him.

Q. Did you?

A. Yes, I did. He showed me pictures of the cars, the news clippings that I never saw. We talked a little bit about things we remembered.

Q. What, if anything, did he say to you about his speed that night?

A. He told me that we were going at least eighty miles an hour when we hit the car.

Q. What else, if anything, did he tell you about that night?

A. Well, he said that he remembered me asking him to

drive his car, and I said: "Yeah, maybe I should have." He said: "Maybe none of this would have happened. Maybe I should have let you driven [sic] my car."

Q. He said that?

A. Yes, he did.

Mark Zimmer could scarcely have asked for a more perfect note on which to end his questioning of Lorraine Cush. "Thank you, Lorraine," he said.

Bob Bryan's cross-examination produced no significant new information except a comment from Lorraine that Glenn had leaned over *often* during their ride to kiss Kristen. When Lorraine stepped from the stand, Zimmer rested the Commonwealth's case. Bryan then moved for dismissal of the most serious charges—homicide by motor vehicle, homicide by motor vehicle while under the influence of alcohol, involuntary manslaughter, and driving under the influence of alcohol—on the ground that Zimmer had failed to prove his case.

"Denied," Judge Conway ruled.

Bryan then called Glenn Evans as the sole defense witness. Facing the prospect of imprisonment, Glenn seemed understandably nervous. He bit at his lower lip and glanced warily about the courtroom as he slid into the witness chair. For the moment at least, there was none of the bravado he often displayed in less ominous settings. But fire would flare in his eyes before he left the stand.

At the outset, Bryan asked Glenn about the trip he had made to Scranton with Mark Ordnung before setting out on the ride with Kristen and her friends. Glenn said he returned from Scranton about nine-thirty that night.

"Up to nine-thirty, have you consumed any alcoholic beverages that day?" Bryan asked.

"Yes, I have," Glenn said. "Between six and nine-thirty, I consumed about four beers. I wasn't sure of how many. I wasn't keeping track or anything."

"Would it have been six beers?"

"No. It could have been four or five, but I know I didn't have a six-pack for sure."

Glenn said he started on another bottle of beer about the time the girls arrived—a time he placed at ten-thirty to ten forty-five. He testified that Kristen brought a beer into the apartment, that he was not sure whether Heidi had one, but that Lorraine did not. When he and the girls left for the ride, he said, he took his beer with him.

"There has been testimony that you were driving down the road with a beer between your legs," Bryan said. "Is that the beer?"

"That was the one," Glenn replied.

Q. There was testimony that you took more than one beer from the house with you. Is that correct?

A. That is correct.

Q. Did you open any of those after you left the house?

A. No, I didn't.

Q. How is it that you came to be in the vehicle this night with the three girls?

A. Well, we wanted to go for a ride. Mark wanted me to go with him, but I didn't want to go with him because he wanted to go to Kuester's and I didn't feel like drinking any more. So he left, okay, then me and the three girls were still there. So I said to Kristen, "You want to go for a ride?" And she said, "Sure." And I said, "You want to go alone?" And she goes, "No, let's get Heidi and Lorraine because they are with me and I don't want to leave them behind." So I said, "Let's go for a little ride and I will have you back, and then I will go to bed and you guys can get home before twelve."

Asked about getting stuck in a ditch during the ride, Glenn shrugged it off as a minor inconvenience. "I gave it two tries and I got it out," he testified. "I didn't have to get out of the car to get it out." Bryan then questioned him about the events leading to the collision, beginning at the point where he passed Michael Madan's car.

"Did you pass that car at a high rate of speed?" Bryan asked.

"I come up on it above the average speed," Glenn said.

"Let's say the car was going fifty-five miles an hour or there-abouts," Bryan suggested.

"I come up on it a little greater of the speed. It wasn't much, and then—"

Bryan, scowling slightly, interrupted his young client. "Glenn, just a minute," he said. "That doesn't really put the football on the field. How much faster than fifty-five were you coming up?"

"I would say ten."

Glenn said he was not looking at his speedometer at the time, and was basing his estimate on the previous testimony that Madan's car was going about fifty-five miles an hour. "I gave it the gas to pass and then I slowed down," he said.

Q. Do you know what your speed was to pass? Greater than sixty-five?

A. Yes.

Q. Greater than eighty?

A. I don't think so. Not at all.

Q. Were you able to get the car completely back into the lane?

A. Yes, I had it back in my lane.

Q. What happened next?

A. We were coming up on the corner after I passed the car. I was slowing down. I was going over the yellow line a little ways—a quarter of a car might have been over—to make the corner.

Q. Are you telling me that you purposely were over the yellow line?

A. I was purposely over to make the corner, yes, and my passenger, Kristen, saw an oncoming car and—

Q. Do you remember if you were kissing Kristen?

A. She was sitting here. We were, like, together. She is over a bit and I was over a bit.

Q. And you said that Kristen saw a car coming? Did you see it?

A. Yes, I did.

Q. Could you give us an idea how many seconds it would have been until the car would have passed you?

A. It could have been five to ten.

Q. What happened when you both saw the car?

A. Well, in fact, I was over the yellow line. And Kristen yelled my name and she yelled: "Glenn, watch it!" And I didn't say anything. I didn't have time to say anything. And the next thing I know she just, like, pulled me back over and she grabbed the wheel and jerked it in a downward motion to bring the car over. I brought it back and, when she pulled it to the right, it went this way and then, when I tried to bring it back, it slid that way. And I knew I couldn't control the car after that, so I just hit the brake. You know, that was it.

Q. Do you remember sliding?

A. I remember going into the slide. I don't remember anything other than that.

Glenn said he did recall riding to the hospital later in an ambulance, passing out, and awakening to find state trooper O'Day waiting to question him. "I asked him how Kristen was doing and he wouldn't tell me," Glenn testified. "I remember Mr. Umstadter walking into my room, and I wanted to talk to him. Mr. O'Day wouldn't let me talk to him. He told Mr. Umstadter, 'Just leave.' And all I remember is him reading my rights and that was it."

In his cross-examination, Mark Zimmer hammered at the point that drinking beer illegally while riding in a car hardly seemed a novel experience for Glenn. After all, by Glenn's own testimony, he had been drinking while riding with Mark Ordnung only hours before the collision that killed Kristen Umstadter.

"Mr. Evans, you had been drinking that evening from six o'clock on, basically?" Zimmer asked.

"Well, six to nine-thirty. I stopped and then I started again when the girls arrived. That is when I opened another beer."

"And that would have been in the maximum your sixth beer?"

"The max, yes."

"You were drinking with your friend Mark Ordnung. You went over to Scranton. Mark Ordnung was driving?"

"He was driving his car," Glenn said.

"You were both drinking on the way over?"

"We both drank. I assume I drank four to five. I know he didn't drink more than three or four."

"He was driving, after all?" Zimmer asked acidly.

"Objection, Your Honor," Bob Bryan interjected. "There is no reason for that comment."

"Sustained," the judge said.

Zimmer, hunting for inconsistencies in Glenn's story, took him back over his testimony that he "didn't feel like drinking any more" when he parted company with Mark Ordnung and went riding with the girls on the night of the accident. "That is right," Glenn reasserted. But if that were the case, Zimmer wanted to know, why did Glenn take beer with him on the fatal ride?

"I had it with me in the car," Glenn said. "I may have taken an occasional drink."

"While you were driving?" Zimmer asked.

"Yes," Glenn conceded.

Q. Did you have both hands on the wheel?

A. Both hands on the wheel until I consumed. I was driving.

Q. And you were driving pretty fast that night, weren't you?

A. At times, yes.

Q. You weren't paying any attention to the speedometer?

A. Not at all.

Q. Were you paying any attention to where the yellow line was in the middle?

A. Yes, I was.

Now, suddenly, Glenn began to show flashes of temper. Zimmer asked whether the road marking at the scene of the collision was a double yellow line.

"I knew what it was," Glenn replied heatedly.

"Mr. Evans, you didn't use very good judgment that night, did you?" Zimmer asked.

"At times, maybe," Glenn said. Then, bristling, he added: "I don't understand what you are trying to say."

"Well, do you think you used good judgment in trying to pass a car on a double yellow line?"

"That isn't good judgment," Glenn admitted.

"Do you think you used good judgment going pretty fast that night?"

"No."

"Do you think you used good judgment in driving with a beer between your legs and sipping from it occasionally?"

"No."

"Yet, at the time you passed that car, the beer was between your legs and you were leaning to your right, the music was loud, and you were going, to use your words, 'a little bit faster than the other car.' You felt you had that car under control, didn't you?"

"Yes, I did."

"Of course," Zimmer said. "And all was right with the world?"

"I ain't saying that," Glenn snapped, his eyes blazing. "I didn't say it was right at all."

"You suddenly realized you couldn't control that car after it jerked to the right?"

"It was jerked to the right," Glenn insisted. "I tried to get it back under control and there was no way. I just hit the brakes and hoped nothing would happen."

"You gave up, is that right?"

"I didn't really give up. I hit the brakes hoping that we would not slide, you know. And, when it started riding this way, I just hit the brakes and I knew there was nothing that could be done."

When Bob Bryan got his shot at redirect questioning, he pressed the contention that blame for the collision could not be placed clearly on Glenn's shoulders. "Glenn, the second before the accident, after you had pulled back in, did you have this car under control before the wheel was touched?" Bryan asked.

"Yes, I did," Glenn replied.

"If the wheel had not been touched and your driving of the car had not been interfered with at this point in time, would you still have had that collision with that car?"

"Your Honor, objection," Mark Zimmer protested. "It is sheer speculation." But before the judge could rule on the objection, Glenn had answered the question.

"I don't think so," he said.

"Why do you think you would not have?" Bryan asked.

"Because I had the car under control after I passed the car, and I had my foot—I was slowing down already and I was coming out of the turn—well, I was coming into the turn and I was in the turn and I was casually bringing it over to my side of the road. And I was just going to continue down the road. I am positive it wouldn't have happened."

Zimmer, on recross-examination, asked: "Glenn, you had it in your control in your judgment, isn't that correct?"

"In whose judgment?"

"*Your* judgment."

"Yes, that is correct."

Zimmer's point was scarcely lost on anyone in the courtroom: Glenn had already admitted his judgment that night had not exactly verged on the infallible. Zimmer had no more questions. Neither did Bryan.

"We rest," Bryan announced.

In his summation, Bryan told the judge the evidence showed "my client was acting like an ass" the night of the collision but not that he was under the influence of alcohol. "The evidence

all shows that the car was driven at a high rate of speed,"
Bryan said. "The car was not, however, driven in an erratic
manner. There was testimony as to being stuck. The way this
occurred, it could have happened to anybody in a situation like
that. In no way does it advance the ball as to whether there was
any showing of intoxication."

Bryan argued that shock resulting from the collision could
have made Glenn appear drunk when he was not. "It does not
appear, Your Honor, on the basis of all the testimony, including
that of the girls who testified here today, that my client consumed so much beer that per se he would have been intoxicated." Bryan did not dispute, however, that Glenn had vio-
lated the law by drinking while driving, carrying open beer
bottles in his car, and driving at an imprudent speed. And he
made only a perfunctory argument against the charge that
Glenn had illegally passed Michael Madan's car.

But as for the accident itself, he pressed Glenn's unsupported
claim that Kristen had grabbed the wheel and he contended the
collision was not Glenn's fault. "This was an internal force
acting on the vehicle by a person other than the person that
should have been controlling the vehicle," Bryan said. "The
accident occurred because of the intervention of Kristen Umstadter and not as a direct result of my client's driving."

Mark Zimmer opened his summation on a personal note.
"Your Honor, I don't believe there is anyone in the Wayne
County Bar who has presented more cases before Your Honor
since you were sitting on the bench than I, and yet I have to say
that this is the saddest case I have ever had to present," he said.

"The Commonwealth is not pleased with the facts in this
case—not because we feel we didn't make out a case but because the story that was told is just awful. Underage drinking,
drinking while driving, and consumption of alcohol just perme-
ate this case from the very beginning. Alcohol influenced the
defendant to the point where he was incapable of safe driving.
Now, the defendant himself admitted to me on cross-examination that he made a poor judgment that night. The defense
admitted that he made poor judgment by admitting to the fact

that he was driving recklessly, that he was beyond the speed limit."

Zimmer said he supposed an argument could be made that Glenn was simply showing off that night for the three girls. "That isn't the testimony here today," he said.

"The testimony here today is simply that we have alcohol from the beginning of the evening to the end of the evening. We have the defendant who admits to having been drinking. A defendant whose eyes were bloodshot. And the two women who were with him, who are still alive to talk about it, say they were afraid. This is the person who was making the judgment calls that night—to drive fast, to drive over the center line, to take his turns wide as he was driving fast, to go off to the berm. Certainly, it seems to me, Your Honor, that on the basis of all the testimony something was affecting this man—something was influencing him to a point where he certainly wasn't driving safely."

Then, Zimmer said, came the events immediately preceding the collision. "Now, this is a man that has a beer between his legs, has been sipping from it. He is driving at a high rate of speed. The music is loud. How many more variables can this man take? He leaned to the right to try to kiss Kristen Umstadter. At this point, the headlights come from V. A. Conrad. One more variable."

The physical evidence, Zimmer said, contradicted Glenn's claim that Kristen had pulled the wheel to the right and caused the accident. "If the actual cause of the accident was a turning to the right, there certainly would not have been a [leftward] spin to come across and leave two hundred and sixteen feet of skid marks," he argued.

"Your Honor, on that basis, I don't believe that there is any question as to who actually caused this accident. I ask for a verdict of guilty on all charges."

Judge Conway said he would review his notes on the case overnight and deliver a verdict at nine-thirty the following morning. It was to prove an emotional night for all the central participants in the trial, but perhaps most emotional—curiously—for Mark Zimmer.

Although he had seemed the quintessentially zealous prosecutor in the courtroom, it developed that Zimmer was tortured by questions about the Evans case. When he reached home that evening, he agonized for hours over the trial. It had been his duty, he knew, to prosecute Glenn Evans. But fulfilling that duty had torn him apart.

"What kind of justice have I worked, if any?" Zimmer asked his wife, Linda. "I've proven my case on all nine counts and now I'm putting a twenty-year-old boy behind bars with hardened criminals. He's going to come out far worse than the night this thing happened. Why? Because society is demanding its pound of flesh. What good does that do anybody? It doesn't bring Kristen Umstadter back."

SEVEN

Mark Zimmer was wrong. He had not proved Glenn Evans guilty on all nine counts—at least not to Judge Robert Conway's satisfaction. But he *had* proved Glenn guilty on seven of the nine counts.

When court reconvened on Wednesday morning, January 21, the judge ruled Zimmer had presented only "sketchy evidence" to support the contention that Glenn's blood-alcohol content had reached the intoxication level at the time of the collision. In the absence of stronger evidence on the point, Conway said, he was compelled to find Glenn not guilty on the charges of driving under the influence of alcohol and homicide by motor vehicle while under the influence.

At the same time, however, the judge held that Glenn's actions that night had been "not only unsafe and negligent but wild"—clearly sufficient to warrant guilty verdicts on the remaining seven counts. Of those, the most serious were homicide by motor vehicle and involuntary manslaughter. Each carried a possible five-year prison sentence and a ten-thousand-dollar fine. The remaining charges on which Glenn was convicted subjected him only to fines ranging from twenty-five to three hundred dollars each. Had he been convicted on the charge of homicide by motor vehicle while under the influence, he would have faced a mandatory minimum sentence of three years and a maximum of seven years.

Judge Conway ordered probation officers to prepare a background report on Glenn and postponed sentencing until the report could be completed. In the meantime, he permitted Glenn to remain free on five thousand dollars' bail.

Glenn fully expected a prison sentence. He was so sure of

doing time that he wrote a farewell letter to his brother Mark after returning home from the courthouse. The letter was to be opened only on the day of Glenn's sentencing.

Although Glenn was younger than Mark, he had been cast in the big-brother role during the time they shared the apartment. That role was reflected in his letter.

"If I don't come home today, I want you to do the following things," Glenn wrote. There followed a list of eleven chores Mark should perform around their apartment.

Then the letter turned to a matter of romance. After Kristen Umstadter's death, Glenn had begun dating a girl named Jeanne Marie Coscia. "I'm going to leave you money," Glenn wrote Mark. "Get Jeanne a dozen roses and have them sent to her house. Put on the card, 'Dear Jeanne: Be strong. I will see you soon. Glenn.' "

The remainder of the letter, marked by occasionally mangled spelling, expressed Glenn's affection for his brother and offered messages to be passed on to other members of the family. "Good luck in the few months ahead," Glenn wrote Mark. "I know it's going to be tough. I wish you all the luck in stratining things out. I know I was always mizzerable and bitchy, but thats because your my brother. I don't want to see you in trouble because I love you."

On the side of the letter, Glenn scrawled: "Mark, I'm counting on you. Tell eveyone that I said goodbye and good luck. Stay out of trouble."

If Glenn had somehow reached a sense of peace with himself, as it seemed, the Umstadters assuredly had not. Glenn's trial had not only failed to answer their questions about the case; it also had created disturbing new issues. Laraine, Dave, Travis, and their friends would never accept that Kristen had pulled the steering wheel, as Glenn claimed. Nor would they accept that Kristen had bought the beer at Kuester's or driven around drinking beer, as Heidi Stacier and Lorraine Cush claimed.

As Travis would put it: "I had so many questions—so many ifs, ands, buts, and whys. . . . Kristen wouldn't even ride in my car when I was drinking. And I couldn't understand that she was out drinking and riding around. It just wasn't her. It wasn't Kristen."

Allan Rutledge, among others, challenged Glenn's story that Kristen had grabbed the steering wheel. "Kristen used to ride with Travis and he would never let anybody touch the wheel," Allan said. "Kristen knew that. So Glenn's story about her grabbing the wheel can't be true. Even riding with me, when we were holding hands and the truck would run off the road, she'd never grab the wheel. She might say something to me—to watch it—but she'd never touch the wheel."

For whatever it was worth, Laraine Umstadter also complained that the roles of Glenn, Heidi, and Lorraine in Kristen's life had been misrepresented at the trial and in the public perception. "Glenn Evans was *not* Kristen's boyfriend," Laraine insisted. "They went to the county fair together, then she baked him a birthday cake, and she saw him the night of the accident. That was it. Those were the only times they did anything together. Kristen just felt sorry for him. And I don't buy the story that Kristen suggested going to Glenn's that night. I think that was somebody else's idea. Before they went to Glenn's, they stopped at McDonald's. I think they met somebody there who suggested they go to Glenn's." Who that somebody might be was another of the Umstadters' unanswered questions. As for Heidi and Lorraine—and why they might have testified as they had about Kristen's buying the beer and drinking it while driving—Laraine said: "They were not Kristen's close friends. They were just school acquaintances."

Beyond that, the Umstadters and their adherents were angered by the outcome of the trial itself. They contended Glenn Evans had gotten off easy by beating the charges of driving under the influence and homicide by motor vehicle while under the influence. And they feared he would also get off easy when the time came for sentencing.

"We heard many stories that he was going to get off," Laraine says. "They knew he was drinking and they knew he was speeding and that he caused this accident. We felt that he should be punished for that."

For the Umstadters, life became what Laraine would call "a nightmare day after day." And for Laraine in particular, that metaphorical nightmare would be compounded by an actual nightmare.

Night after night, it would torment her. She would lie in bed and try to unwind—a jumble of discordant thoughts surging through her mind. Somehow, at last, sleep would come. And then the nightmare.

Laraine would see and hear it all: Glenn Evans's Duster speeding past Michael Madan's car on Route 652. The lights of the approaching station wagon popping over the hill. Kristen screaming. Glenn swerving into the other lane. His wheels hitting the shoulder. The Duster sliding into a skid, then a spin. The horrible, bone-crushing crash. *And, through it all, Laraine would be sitting right there in the car with Kristen!*

Unlike the typical nightmare, this one would yield no sense of relief in its aftermath. For, each time Laraine awoke, she would be confronted with the reality that Kristen had actually died out there on the highway—not merely in some recurring dream.

That reality compelled the Umstadters to continue seeking answers to their multitude of questions. Since Glenn Evans's trial had not produced answers—or, at least, the answers they wanted—they clung to their ritual of endlessly reexamining the case around the kitchen table each evening. Laraine continued pressing Travis to seek information from his friends.

"My mother every day was asking me what did I hear, what did I find out," Travis would recall. "Asking me these questions. And every day she asked me. Every day I felt smaller because she was leaning on her son for something and I couldn't give it."

The Umstadters' frustration, in turn, fueled their indignation. Bitter, angry words—usually directed at Glenn—often flew across the kitchen table.

"I'd like to see Glenn's bones crushed in a car-crusher at a wrecking yard the way Kristen's bones were crushed in the accident," Laraine said one night. She insisted later that she did not mean it literally, that she had made the remark the way an irritated parent might tell a child: "I'll kill you." But she conceded she had developed an abiding animosity toward Glenn.

Although the Umstadters had no way of knowing it at the time, Glenn himself was belatedly expressing remorse over Kristen's death during that period. True, it may well have been a self-serving remorse. But the person to whom he expressed it thought not.

Chief Wayne County probation officer Linus Myers—the man who had taught the underage-drinking course Travis Umstadter had been required to attend as a teenager—was now preparing the presentence probation report on Glenn Evans. Within days of Judge Conway's verdict, Myers drove out to Glenn's apartment to interview him.

Glenn told still again his story that Kristen had grabbed the steering wheel. But he acknowledged that he had been driving recklessly and had been responsible for the collision.

"I wish I could right what I've done," Glenn said. "I realize there's no way I can do that. I'm sorry for what happened, but I'm trying to put it behind me."

Glenn told Myers he knew he was going to serve time, that he was prepared for it and planning to go on with his life from there. "That's all I can do," he said.

Myers concluded Glenn was sincere. The tall, slender probation officer was struck—as high school principal Dan O'Neill had been—by the strong similarities between Glenn and Travis. "They seemed very much alike in personality, temperament, and interests," Myers would recall. "I formed a liking for both of them."

After asking Glenn the usual biographical questions—family background, education, employment history—Myers decided the young man had done pretty well for himself, all things considered, until the fatal collision. "You have to remember his parents split up when he was young," Myers says. "He was out on his own, living with his brother. He finished high school. He enrolled in that automotive-mechanics' school. And he'd never been in any trouble before the accident."

Myers did not immediately reach a decision on what sentence to recommend for Glenn. But he was certain it would be less than the five-year maximum prison term. It would be up to Judge Conway to decide whether to accept the eventual recommendation.

Before leaving Glenn's apartment, Myers said: "There's a lot of talk that Travis has threatened you. Is there anything to that?"

"He hasn't made any direct threats," Glenn replied. But he said that when they encountered each other around town Travis would form a mock pistol with his thumb and index finger—the way kids do—and pretend to shoot him: Bang! Bang!

The truth of it was that talk of impending trouble between the Umstadter and Evans camps was all over town. Allan Rutledge said more than once: "Glenn ought to be killed." Other friends of Travis and Kristen said Glenn did not deserve to live. Glenn's friends, for their part, were making bellicose noises of their own.

Time, it seemed, was not healing *these* wounds. Each day, positions hardened. Each day, nerves were jangled. Each day, the tension grew more conspicuously palpable.

One afternoon, Travis was driving along Main Street with a friend, Tom Frisch, when they spotted Glenn in his new car. Glenn was jerking the car erratically—first mashing the gas pedal, then the brake pedal—and laughing all the while. Seeing Glenn drive that way, after what had happened to Kristen, infuriated Travis anew.

"He's an asshole," Travis said. "I'd like to kill him."

Tom Frisch said he'd like to kill Glenn, too.

It was Saturday night, January 24, four days after Glenn's trial. Travis was drinking in a bar called Cheers just across the state line in Cochecton, New York. Another friend, Doug Smith, was with him.

Dougie Smith, as their crowd called him, had run with Travis since the fourth grade. Trained as a diesel mechanic, he was now working for an excavating company. He was short and thin, with long brown hair, a stringy mustache, and a stubble of chin fuzz.

As they had done many times, Travis and Dougie drifted into a dark conversation about Kristen's death. Dougie shared Travis's fear that Glenn would be let off easy in court. He had told Travis repeatedly that he would like to "get" Glenn. Now Travis was talking about how much he missed Kristen.

"I'm going to get even," Travis said. "Glenn won't live until spring."

It was Monday, January 26. Glenn Evans was meeting with Bob Bryan in the lawyer's office to discuss the impending sentencing.

"Travis is gonna kill me," Glenn said.

"What do you mean?"

"He keeps going by and pointing his finger at me like it's a gun."

"Stay away from him," Bryan said.

Later that day, on the courthouse steps, Bryan encountered Lee Krause—the lawyer representing the Umstadter family in civil claims resulting from Kristen's death. Bryan said Glenn felt Travis was threatening him.

"I'm hearing just the opposite," Krause told him.

It was Tuesday, January 27. Dave Umstadter had been brooding about Glenn Evans. Now that the trial was over—and it seemed Glenn might get off with a light sentence—Dave could restrain himself no longer. He sat down and wrote a letter telling Glenn what he thought of him:

> You don't seem to have any idea what you have done to me and my family. We loved Kristen. She was our own pride and joy.
>
> You took her life and you don't even seem to care. Do you think you're a big macho man?
>
> I wish you were dead.

Dave put a stamp on the letter and dropped it in the mail.

That same day, shortly before 7:30 A.M., Travis had left the family home on Erie Street and walked down the hill to the entrance to Moore Business Forms. He was working at the time for a company called Kramer's Framers, constructing the wooden frames for new homes being built in a section of Wayne County called the Hideout. Travis and a coworker, a childhood friend named Randy Young, took turns driving to the job site each day. Since this was Randy's day, he picked Travis up in front of Moore's and they rode to the Hideout—making small talk.

It was 4:00 P.M. Travis and Randy knocked off work early. Ordinarily they stayed until six o'clock. But Tuesday was Randy's bowling night, so he customarily quit a couple of hours early. Travis, with no other way to get home, left early as well.

When Randy dropped him off, Travis found nobody at the Umstadter home. He went to the kitchen, made a peanut butter and jelly sandwich, and hastily gobbled it down. His father had mentioned that he might do some sheetrock work that afternoon at the big new house the family was building in the Duck Harbor Pond section near Lookout. Travis decided to ride out to the house and see if he could help.

He drove through Honesdale, then north on Highway 191, and cut left at the turnoff to Duck Harbor Pond. But when Travis reached the new house, Dave was not there.

So he drove to the Mountain View bar in Lookout. The Mountain View, one of Travis's hangouts, was an old white-frame roadhouse on the west side of Highway 191. Out in back of the place sat an array of aging cars and trucks. The establishment's main room offered, aside from the bar, such secondary attractions as a pool table, a jukebox, and a collection of game machines. Above the door hung a mounted deer head with a pool cue perched between its antlers.

Behind the bar was a sign bearing a sketch of a shotgun. "This house guarded by shotgun three nights per week," the sign said. "You guess which three."

Tending bar was a slim, pretty blonde named Sherry Dennis, whose family operated the Mountain View. She had known Travis since grade school. Travis asked to use the phone behind the bar and called home. His father answered. Travis explained that they had missed connections at the new house.

"I'm going to be out for a while," Travis said. "Tell Mom not to fix supper for me."

"Okay," Dave told him. "Just be careful. Don't come in too late."

"All right."

Travis spotted another familiar face. Cord Meyer, a friend who had also known him since grade school, was seated on a stool near the middle of the bar. Travis took a stool beside him.

Cord was buying. Travis started with a shot of apple schnapps. During the next hour, Cord bought him another half-dozen shots of schnapps. Travis washed them down with beer.

It had been months since Cord had seen Travis. "I'm really sorry about Kristen," Cord said. "You know how much I cared for her. If I can do anything for you or your family, give me a call."

Travis thanked him, but they immediately changed the subject. Neither wanted to talk about anything that would depress them. They shifted instead into desultory barroom talk—what was going on in Travis's life, what was going on in Cord's.

It was 7:00 P.M. Cord had to leave. "I'm already running late," he said. His father's cows needed milking.

When Cord had gone, Travis asked Sherry Dennis if he could use the phone again.

"Go ahead," she said.

Travis called Dougie Smith at home. "Want to go on a road trip?" he asked.

"Sure," Dougie said. "But I don't have any money."

"Don't worry about it," Travis said. "I'm buying. I'll pick you up."

Travis bought two six-packs of Genessee, carried them to his car, and drove the two miles to Dougie's house. Dougie was waiting with three bottles of Budweiser in hand. He slid into the front passenger seat of Travis's gray and white Pontiac Bonneville.

The two of them cruised the back roads for about three hours—riding aimlessly, talking, and drinking the beer—from the north end of Wayne County clear to the south end and back. They stopped along the way at a Honesdale bar called the Limerick and bought still another six-pack. Between them, during the ride, they polished off eighteen bottles of beer.

It had snowed earlier. When Dougie and Travis rolled into the access area at Lake Wallenpaupack, they found that the lower level of the two-tier parking lot had been plowed but the upper level had not. Travis cruised to the far end of the lower level, then turned and paused to deliberate whether they could return through the snow on the upper level.

"Think we can make it?" he asked.

"Yeah, go for it," Dougie said.

Travis went for it. He didn't make it. Within seconds the car was stuck in a pile of snow. Shifting the car forward and backward, he eventually pulled it loose. He and Dougie drank some more beer and went on their way, driving off through the woods surrounding the lake.

Suddenly a deer burst out of the woods and ran into the roadway. Travis jammed on the brakes. His handgun—the single-action, .22-caliber revolver his father had bought him as a Christmas present thirteen months earlier—slid out from the spot beneath the car seat where Travis habitually kept it ready for hunting and trapping. Travis managed to dodge the deer. But the gun came to rest between the gas and brake pedals, interfering with his driving. He reached down, grabbed the gun, and shoved it back under the seat.

A short time later, Travis applied the brakes, and the gun again slid out from beneath the seat. He picked it up and put it on the seat beside him. The revolver was inside a black leather holster.

Just a few miles down the road, another deer jumped out in front of the car. Again Travis jammed on the brakes. The gun tumbled from the seat to the floor. Dougie retrieved it and placed it back on the seat.

Although it was only a little past ten o'clock, Dougie was winding down. He was feeling the beer, the fatigue, and the stuffiness of the car. Travis drove back past Lookout to Equinunk, where Dougie lived, and dropped him off at his house. For lack of anything better to do, Travis then returned to the Mountain View bar.

It was 10:30 P.M. Sherry Dennis's brother Clint was now tending bar at the Mountain View. Clint had known Travis since the seventh grade. As kids they often had driven an old Volkswagen around a field behind the Umstadter home. They also had occasionally hunted together.

Clint served Travis a bottle of Genessee and asked what was new. Travis allowed that he and Chrissy Striffler were talking about getting married.

"You're nuts!" Clint told him. "You're too young to get married."

Travis endured the needling, talked to Clint a bit, fed quarters into the jukebox—strictly for country-and-western songs—and then moved down the bar to sit with a friend named Dave Pallis. He and Dave talked for more than an hour. Travis drank another three beers.

He seemed happy-go-lucky at first, mentioning his marriage plans and shrugging off the obligatory smartass remarks. But then Kristen's name came up, and Travis's mood turned darker.

Kristen didn't drink, Travis said, no matter what the testimony claimed at Glenn Evans's trial. Now she was dead, and he missed her terribly.

"It isn't fair," Travis said.

His face turned red. His eyes filled with tears. Dave Pallis tried to change the subject and cheer Travis up. But it didn't work.

Travis set his half-filled beer bottle on the bar. Then, despite all the drinking he had done, he walked toward the door without displaying any sign of unsteadiness. He glanced at the clock behind the bar and noticed that it was almost twelve-thirty.

Back in his car, Travis headed south on Highway 191 toward home. His eyes were still misty, and he was steering with difficulty. Between Lookout and Honesdale he drove into a pile of snow and almost became stuck once more. He spun the wheels back and forth, managing to pull free. But the gun fell off the seat again, landing near the pedals and sliding partially out of the holster.

Annoyed, Travis reached down, tossed the holster aside, and picked up the revolver. He was wearing two layers of flannel shirts, one hanging down outside his pants. Pulling up the outer shirt, he stuffed the gun into the waistband of his pants.

As he drove, he brooded about Kristen and the unfairness of it all. Now he was rolling down Honesdale's Main Street—past the traffic light at the intersection of Route 6, past the darkened stores, past the Farmers and Merchants Bank. The downtown traffic lights were flashing yellow caution signals, as they always did after midnight. Travis was about five blocks from home.

But Kristen was still hanging over him. During the coming day, Travis knew, his parents would ask him still again whether he had heard anything new about Kristen's death. He had been out half the night. And still he had no answers for his family.

Travis abruptly swung his car to the left, made a U-turn, and headed back to the north on Main Street. When he reached Route 6, he turned left past the old Wayne Hotel and Wayne County Memorial Hospital.

A few minutes later he made a right turn off the highway, then another quick right into the parking lot behind the Buckley Building—the old barn converted into a small apartment house. Unsure which apartment he wanted, he walked toward the one apartment where lights were still burning. The apartment stood in the center of the building. On its door hung a metal number three.

Travis knocked at Glenn Evans's front door.

EIGHT

Glenn Evans was talking on the telephone to his girlfriend, Jeanne Marie Coscia, when Travis Umstadter came to the door. Jeanne Marie had seen Glenn only a short time earlier—she had stopped at his apartment on the way back from a ski trip—but they had nonetheless been talking on the phone now for almost an hour. Glenn's brother Mark was asleep in the upstairs bedroom, apparently oblivious to the noise from a radio blaring just a few feet from his pillow.

There was a loud thumping sound. "I think someone's at the door," Glenn told Jeanne Marie. "Hold on a minute."

After a pause, Jeanne Marie heard Glenn ask: "What the hell are you doing here?"

He then returned to the phone and told her: "Travis Umstadter's here, and it looks like he's gonna kick my ass."

"Wake Mark up," Jeanne Marie urged.

"Call me back in an hour, and I'll let you know what happened," Glenn said.

Jeanne Marie stretched out on a couch at her home, a portable phone beside her. But shortly she fell asleep.

Glenn led Travis from the door to the center of the combination living room/dining area/kitchen that made up the apartment's entire first floor. A staircase to the left of the doorway rose to the second-floor bedroom and bathroom.

"I knew it was gonna come to this sooner or later," Glenn said.

He pulled out a chair at an oval table in the dining area. "Have a seat," Glenn said.

The two of them, both noticeably nervous, sat at the table—

Travis with his back to the door, Glenn to his right. "Want a beer?" Glenn asked.

"No, I've had enough already tonight," Travis said. Glenn laughed.

Travis pulled out a pack of Marlboro Lights and set them on the table. Each of them drew a cigarette from the pack and lighted up.

"Glenn, there is no judge here," Travis said. "There is no jury. Forget that I'm Kristen's brother. Just talk to me."

"I knew we had to talk," Glenn said. "I'm glad you came."

"Tell me what really happened," Travis said. "Your trial is over. What you testified to and what you were tried for, you can't be tried again. My family and I have a right. We need to know what happened."

They talked for more than an hour, each reaching over now and then to take another cigarette from Travis's pack. The conversation was civil enough at first. Glenn did tell Travis about the events leading to the accident and about the collision itself. But there was nothing new in his account. It simply mirrored the testimony at his trial.

Travis was not getting the answers he wanted. The longer they talked, the more frustrated he became. Neither Glenn nor Travis raised his voice or showed open anger. But the civility between them dissolved—to be succeeded by biting sarcasm. Travis accused Glenn of offering smartass answers that were not true.

"Glenn, I'm asking you one more time, tell me the truth," Travis said.

"I don't know why you bother me with this," Glenn snapped. "If that dumb bitch sister of yours hadn't grabbed the steering wheel, she would be living today."

Travis could barely contain himself. But Glenn was not finished. "I'm sick and tired of the looks I'm getting from people around town," he said. "I'm sick and tired of the remarks—the rumors I'm hearing about people wanting to come after me. I'm gonna stop it. And I'm gonna stop it with you."

Now both of them were suddenly rising from their chairs.

It was shortly after 2:00 A.M. Jack Rickert, a carpenter who lived in the apartment next door to Glenn and Mark Evans, was jarred from sleep by a sharp succession of loud banging noises. He thought someone was beating on a wall inside the Evans apartment. Then he heard a thumping sound, as if someone had fallen or a piece of furniture had toppled over next door. Next there was the sound of the front door slamming shut in the Evans apartment. Finally, Rickert heard a car pulling out of the parking lot, churning up gravel.

Rickert was accustomed to noise from the next apartment. He had complained constantly about the Evans brothers' noisy parties and loud music. Thus, after hearing the car drive away, he rolled over and went back to sleep—grateful that he still had four hours before his alarm clock would wake him for work.

It was 2:30 A.M. Travis pulled his car into the driveway outside the house on Erie Street. He tripped slightly climbing the outside stairs, but righted himself and reached for the front doorknob. There was a slight squeak as the knob turned.

"Mom!" Travis screamed. "Mom! Oh, my God! Oh, my God! Mom! Mom!"

He was sobbing as he rushed up the staircase to the second floor. Laraine and Dave, abruptly awakened by his arrival, met him at the landing. Laraine asked what was wrong, but Travis continued to cry. Even when she shook him by the shoulders, she could not get Travis to tell her what had happened.

The three of them trooped downstairs to the kitchen, where Laraine brewed a pot of coffee. Travis reeked of alcohol. His eyes were bloodshot. Again Laraine asked him: "What happened?"

"I went to see Glenn Evans," Travis said. "I think he may be hurt."

Then he burst into sobs again. He sagged into a chair, put his head on the kitchen table, and cried uncontrollably—his body trembling. Dave, Jr., awakened by the commotion, came downstairs and tried to comfort his kid brother. But Travis simply continued to cry.

For the short term at least, he seemed incapable of providing

a coherent account of what had happened. Laraine handed him
a cup of coffee. He drank it down and asked for more. The sobs
persisted. But intermittently Travis would blurt a word or two.
Once he made an oblique reference to his gun.

So now he had mentioned the gun, going to see Glenn Evans,
and that Glenn might be hurt. That was enough for Laraine.
Her experience as a legal secretary told her it was time to call in
an attorney.

The attorney then representing the Umstadter family, Lee
Krause, had an unlisted home telephone number. But Laraine
was frantic by that time. She also was resourceful. Minutes
later, Krause was awakened by the ringing of the telephone
near his bed.

"Hello," he muttered.

"This is the telephone-company operator," said the woman
on the other end. "Is this Lee Krause?"

"Yes."

"I have an emergency call for you. Do you want me to put it
through?"

"Who's calling?"

"Laraine Umstadter."

"Sure, put her on."

Laraine told Krause what little she knew—explaining that
Travis had been drinking, was hysterical, and was not talking
coherently. Krause said he would be right over but also would
have to call the police.

After they had hung up, Krause called the Honesdale barracks of the state police. Trooper Andrew Piezga came on the
line. Krause told him one of his clients might have been involved in a shooting. He suggested that the trooper meet him at
the Umstadter home. But since Piezga was unfamiliar with the
Umstadters' neighborhood, they agreed to meet nearby instead
—at the entrance to Moore Business Forms.

Piezga and another trooper, Robert Fuehrer, rode to Moore's
in a state police Jeep to wait for Krause. Somehow Krause and
the troopers missed connections. Krause drove on to the Umstadter home. He conferred briefly with the Umstadters, advis-

ing all of them against making statements to the authorities, then called the state police barracks again. Eventually a Honesdale policeman named Gus Nearing happened along and led the troopers to the house. Krause met them outside.

He told them it appeared that his client, whom he did not immediately identify, might have been involved in a shooting. Krause said he had advised the entire family against making statements. He then led the officers into the house, where Travis was still seated at the kitchen table. His head was down. He was crying. His father was holding his hand.

Trooper Fuehrer, tagging every base, read all four of the Umstadters their rights. Krause told Fuehrer that the shooting —if there had been one—apparently had taken place at Glenn Evans's apartment. He suggested the officers check the apartment to determine whether Glenn was all right. But looking toward a possible defense in case this night's events should find their way to court, Krause also requested that Travis be taken to a hospital immediately for a blood-alcohol test.

Once the alcohol issue was raised, Bob Fuehrer decided to perform a simple check of his own on Travis's condition. Fuehrer, forty-five, a chunky, balding man who looked as if he would make a perfect Santa Claus, stepped up to Travis and asked softly: "What's your name, son?"

"Travis Umstadter."

"How do you spell Umstadter?"

"U-M-S-T-A-D-T-E-R."

"What's your date of birth?"

"October thirtieth, 1966."

Officers Piezga and Nearing took Travis to Wayne County Memorial Hospital in the Honesdale police car. Dave Umstadter rode with them. At the same time, Fuehrer and Krause rode to Glenn's apartment in the state police Jeep.

It was 4:10 A.M. Fuehrer peered into Glenn's downstairs room through a pane of glass in the front door. He could see a form on the floor, partly beneath the table. The trooper tried the door, found it unlocked, and opened it. He stepped inside, with Krause directly behind him.

Pointing to a corner of the room, Fuehrer told Krause: "Please, stand over there and don't touch anything." Krause complied.

Glenn Evans was lying on the floor on his back, wearing a T-shirt and slacks but no shoes or socks. Fuehrer knelt beside him and felt for a pulse. Negative. He felt for a heartbeat. Negative. He checked for other vital signs. Negative.

Lights were burning in the room, but not brightly enough for Fuehrer's purpose. He beamed his flashlight on Glenn's face. The eyes were partly open. Fuehrer could see a black spot surrounding a bullet hole over the left eye. When he checked the carotid artery, he spotted a hole in Glenn's neck. There were two more bullet holes—both behind the left ear. Blood was splashed on the table, the floor, and the nearest wall.

Although it hardly needed saying, Fuehrer nonetheless told Krause: "He's dead."

Lee Krause, a trim, precise man of forty, was one of Wayne County's leading criminal and civil lawyers. But his range of experience had not prepared him for this extraordinary night. "How many lawyers call the police to report shootings?" he would later ask. "How many lawyers are on the scene when bodies are discovered? That happens on *Perry Mason,* not in real life. But here it was happening to me."

Bob Fuehrer searched the apartment. He climbed the stairs, opened the bedroom door, and came upon Mark Evans still sleeping with the radio blaring nearby. Mark had slept right through the gunfire. The sound of the shots apparently had been drowned out by the radio. Fuehrer decided not to disturb Mark for the time being. When Mark awoke later, he seemed so genuinely shaken by his brother's death that the authorities never considered him a possible suspect in the shooting.

Fuehrer, after completing his search of the apartment, telephoned his barracks and set the wheels in motion for a full murder investigation. The coroner, crime-scene experts, and an assortment of other investigators were called out of bed and directed to assemble at Glenn's apartment.

By 4:40 A.M., Herman Todd had arrived. A muscular six-footer with the build of a fullback, Todd had been a state police officer for nineteen years—thirteen of them at the Honesdale barracks. Unlike Fuehrer and Piezga, who wore the gray and black of uniformed Pennsylvania troopers, Todd worked in plainclothes. He was a criminal investigator. And he was about to take charge of what would become the most celebrated investigation of his career—indeed, the most celebrated criminal case in Wayne County history.

Fuehrer briefed Todd on what he knew. "I haven't found a weapon," he said.

Krause, overhearing the conversation, broke in to say: "If you search a gray Pontiac parked in front of the Umstadter home, you may find a weapon there."

Next, Fuehrer telephoned District Attorney Ray Hamill. When he heard the phone ring, Hamill assumed it would be Fuehrer calling. Hell, it *always* seemed to be Bob Fuehrer—the mainstay of the state police midnight shift—who woke Hamill in the middle of the night.

"We've got a shooting," Fuehrer said. "It looks like a homicide."

"Okay."

"The victim is Glenn Evans."

"I didn't understand you," Hamill said. "What did you say?"

"The victim is Glenn Evans," Fuehrer repeated.

"Holy shit!" Hamill shouted.

Fuehrer gave him a quick rundown. "Attorney Krause is here with me," he said. Hamill could hear Krause's voice in the background: "Hello, Ray."

Hamill remembers asking himself: What's going on here? One advantage a DA usually enjoys is the opportunity to see a crime scene first and interview witnesses—observing their behavior—before the defense attorneys get to them. And here was a defense attorney on the scene before the DA, greeting him on the phone. It all seemed bizarre.

When Fuehrer told him that Krause had suggested searching Travis's car for the weapon, Hamill ordered: "Don't search it until we can get a warrant. Put someone on the car and don't let anybody get near it." Immediately afterward, an officer was assigned to guard the car.

Ray Hamill hurriedly dressed and kissed his wife, Donna, goodbye. "I'll be back," he said. He did not say he would be back soon. An energetic amateur basketball player even at the age of thirty-six, Hamill recognized from the outset that he was playing catch-up ball in this case. He took off for Glenn Evans's apartment, determined at least to get into the flow of the game.

It was 4:33 A.M. At Wayne County Memorial Hospital, a laboratory technician inserted a hypodermic needle into Travis Umstadter's arm and drew two vials of blood. The vials were turned over to Trooper Piezga. Officers Piezga and Nearing then took Travis and his father to the police barracks. The vials of blood were placed in a refrigerator at the barracks and later transported to the central state police laboratory in Harrisburg. There a police chemist would determine that the blood-alcohol content measured .13—well above the .10 intoxication level.

Investigator Todd and District Attorney Hamill familiarized themselves with the evidence at the Evans apartment, then drove to the police barracks. Lee Krause and Laraine Umstadter also had arrived there. Laraine had been asked to bring Travis a change of clothes because the police wanted to conduct tests on the clothing he had worn during the night.

They all gathered in a large room where troopers usually congregated between patrols. Travis was seated, with his parents standing protectively behind him, when Hamill entered the room. "You could just sense the continuing tragedy of the whole thing," Hamill would recall. Hamill, of course, had dealt with the Umstadters during the Glenn Evans prosecution. He had known Laraine even before that. In fact, he had once contemplated offering her a job as a legal secretary in his private law office. But Hamill now regarded such considerations as irrelevant. He had the murder case of his career to solve and prosecute.

When Herman Todd asked Travis to hand over the clothes he had been wearing, Travis pointed to an outer shirt he had slipped on just before leaving home for the hospital. "Do you want this?" Travis asked. "I wasn't wearing it at the time." He did not elaborate on what he meant by "at the time," but his implication seemed clear. Todd took the shirt just in case it might have picked up some stray piece of evidence.

Although Krause continued to insist that the Umstadters make no statements, he did permit Travis to submit to various police tests. Travis's clothing was tested for blood stains, fibers, and other clues but provided no useful evidence. A sample of his hair was taken for comparison with any hairs that might be found in Glenn's apartment.

John Fox, a state police identification expert, performed the opening stage of a neutron-activation test intended to determine whether Travis had recently fired a gun. Fox applied a 5-percent solution of nitric acid to Travis's hands, then wiped it off with cotton swabs. Later neutron-activation analysis at the lab might detect the presence of barium and antimony in the test swabs—indicating Travis had fired a gun—but the procedure would work only if certain kinds of ammunition had been used. And the police did not yet know what kind of ammunition had killed Glenn Evans.

Hamill was preparing an application for a warrant to search Travis's car when Krause told him that would not be necessary. Both Travis and Krause signed a waiver permitting the authorities to search the car without a warrant.

Todd went to the Umstadter home and checked the Pontiac. He found Travis's gun on the floor, near the driver's side of the front seat. The holster was on the seat. Todd confiscated the gun, the holster, a rubber floor mat, and a wad of paper towels stuffed beneath the front seat. He suspected the mat and the towels might bear chemical residues that could help prove the gun had recently been fired.

The gold-trimmed .22-caliber Excam revolver bore the serial number B58944. A records check on that number determined the gun had been sold on December 11, 1985, by Jerry's Sports Shop in Olyphant, Pennsylvania, to the Lookout General Store. The records showed that Dave and Laraine Umstadter were

registered as federally licensed firearms dealers authorized to
sell guns at the Lookout General Store. They also disclosed
that Dave and Laraine were identified as the current registered
owners of the revolver.

Assuming this revolver indeed proved to be the murder
weapon, investigators reasoned from the beginning, the killer
must have exercised at least a measure of deliberation in committing the crime. The gun's single-action mechanism—making
it necessary for a shooter first to pull back the hammer and
then squeeze the trigger on each shot—seemed to lead inescap-
ably to that conclusion. After all, there were four bullet
wounds. With two hand movements needed to fire each bullet,
the killer would have been required to perform at least eight
distinct acts in carrying out the crime.

Within hours of the shooting, probation officer Linus Myers
was awakened by a phone call from his father, Franklin J. Myers. The elder Myers owned the Franklin J. Myers Funeral
Home in Honesdale. On occasion he called on his son for help
in transporting a body.

"Can you give me a hand this morning?" Franklin Myers
asked.

"Sure."

Franklin Myers, driving his hearse, picked Linus up a short
time later at his home. He mentioned that they were on a police
call.

"Who are we picking up?" Linus asked.

"I don't know. They didn't give me a name, just an address."

As they rode along, it dawned on Linus Myers that he had
driven this same route only a few days earlier—visiting Glenn
Evans's apartment to interview him for the presentencing report. Suddenly he knew what had happened to Glenn. He just
knew.

Linus said nothing but remembers thinking: Oh, shit!

When he and his father reached the apartment, sure enough,
there was Glenn's body stretched out on the floor. There was
no body bag—simply Glenn in plain view, bullet holes clearly
visible. Linus spilled out the story to his father. Even for two

men whose lines of work had accustomed them to jolts, these circumstances stretched far beyond the norm. Shaking their heads, the father and son loaded the body into the hearse and rode away.

It was 8:00 A.M. Jeanne Marie Coscia had slept through the night without trying to call Glenn Evans to check on his encounter with Travis Umstadter. After awakening, she followed her daily routine—eating breakfast, dressing and riding off to Honesdale High School. Now, from the school, she put in a call to Glenn's apartment. A policeman answered. It was from him that Jeanne Marie heard the news that Glenn was dead.

She cried for twenty minutes. Then she telephoned her mother and told her both of Glenn's death and of her conversation with him the previous night. Her mother immediately called the police.

Glenn's mother, Eva Furk, learned of his death while in a rehabilitation center as a result of the automobile accident that had made her a paraplegic. Her son Mark telephoned with the news. For neither the first nor the last time in her life, Eva Furk said: "This family—it's cursed."

Glenn's defense attorney, Bob Bryan, got the word in a telephone call from Ray Hamill. "It wiped me out," Bryan recalls. "Just a few days before, Glenn had been sitting there in a chair right across from me in my office—telling me he was going to get killed. And now he was dead."

At about 2:00 P.M., Wayne County coroner Young W. Lee began an autopsy on Glenn's body in a back room of the Franklin J. Myers Funeral Home. Lee eventually recovered all four bullets from the body, but two were badly mutilated. He found powder burns around several of the wounds, indicating that the shots had been fired at close range. And he concluded that every one of the shots would have been fatal, since all of them passed through a vital section of the brain. Glenn could have lived only for seconds after being struck by the first shot.

Within hours of Glenn Evans's death, Ray Hamill and the state troopers had strong reasons for identifying Travis Umstadter as the chief target of their investigation—reasons beginning with such fundamentals as the Umstadters' role in reporting the shooting and Jeanne Marie Coscia's account of her telephone conversation with Glenn. Still, Hamill did not believe he was anywhere close to ordering an arrest, for a great deal of evidence remained to be gathered and evaluated. Investigators were trying to identify fingerprints found in the Evans apartment. Ballistics tests intended to identify the murder weapon had not yet been performed. Dozens of potential witnesses, including friends of both Glenn and Travis, would have to be interviewed.

Perhaps most important, Hamill and the troopers did not have any direct evidence placing Travis in Glenn's apartment at the time of the shooting. Thus far, at least, there was no physical evidence to prove his presence. Travis and his family were rigidly obeying Lee Krause's instructions to refrain from making statements to the authorities.

Jeanne Marie Coscia's recollection of her telephone conversation with Glenn was hearsay that might or might not be admissible at a trial. In any event, it was not direct evidence. And even if accepted as hearsay evidence, it would indicate only that Travis had come to the apartment during the phone conversation—not necessarily that he had been there when the shooting occurred more than an hour later.

Hamill was well aware, moreover, that Travis had been far from the only person in Wayne County known to be nursing a grudge against Glenn Evans. Thus he could not focus his investigation on Travis to the exclusion of all other possibilities.

If Hamill needed any reinforcement of that position, he received it before the day was out. That afternoon, Glenn's regular mail delivery arrived at his apartment. It was seized for investigation by the state police.

Among the confiscated items was the angry letter written to Glenn by Dave Umstadter. Such a letter, written to a murder victim the day before his death, was hard to ignore. Especially difficult to ignore was the letter's tag line: "I wish you were dead."

NINE

The shock inflicted by Glenn Evans's murder—coming as a sequel to the jolting death of Kristen Umstadter—tore at the very soul of life in Honesdale.

Wayne County averaged just one homicide a year. Typically, local killings were of the ilk derided in some quarters as mere "misdemeanor murders"—the mundane residue of domestic altercations and barroom scrapes. They rated a few sentences of conversation at the dinner table, if that.

But now *everyone* was talking about the Glenn Evans murder. Everyone knew the Umstadter or Evans families. Everyone had an opinion. And a great many people, for a diversity of reasons, were angry about the case.

Some were angry that such a murder, which they assumed from the start to be an act of revenge, could have been committed in this locale. This was not, after all, Dodge City or Tombstone. By God, this was Honesdale, Pennsylvania. And Honesdale, it was said, would not tolerate vigilante justice.

Others were angry because the Evans murder would inevitably give Honesdale a bad name. The news media were bound to play up the angles that would cast the town in the worst light —underage drinking, wild driving, rampaging youth, senseless violence. Not only would all of this be bad for the town's general image, it also would be bad for business in a community already struggling to fight off a succession of economic troubles.

There were those who were angry because they believed the murder could have been prevented. Anyone with eyes and ears, they said, could have seen trouble coming. Why didn't anybody do anything about it?

Lines of contention were drawn between those who abhorre‹ the killing and those who justified it. One side contended Glen‹ Evans got exactly what he deserved: He had taken Kristen' life, had demonstrated no remorse, and had seemed certain t‹ get off with an inconsequential sentence. The other side argue‹ that nothing justified murder and nobody had the right, in ‹ phrase that was heard all over town, "to take the law into hi‹ own hands."

Some attributed the murder, at least in part, to class distinc‹ tions. The Umstadters, it was said, had not considered Glen‹ good enough for Kristen. That's why, after Kristen's death, they had insisted Glenn had not been her boyfriend. The Um‹ stadters resented Glenn, it was argued, and that resentment‹ helped establish the climate leading to the murder.

Conversely, the Umstadters themselves were resented by some because they were transplants. Glenn Evans had lived in Wayne County all his life. That was all certain people wanted to know.

When Travis Umstadter remained at large in the immediate aftermath of the murder, there were complaints that he was receiving favored treatment. He was, after all, represented by Lee Krause, who had been chosen by the Umstadters for his reputation as a trial lawyer but who also was known as an influential figure around town. And some contended Travis was receiving special treatment as well because his mother worked for another attorney.

Linda Soden, deputy clerk in the prothonotary's office at the courthouse, heard "a lot of people saying they were upset with the Commonwealth." Her colleague at the prothonotary's office, Joan Shaffer, detected a widespread perception that Laraine Umstadter was trying to dictate the course of the investigation: "She was insisting from the start, 'Travis is not going to say anything until he talks to an attorney. This is the way it's going to be—one, two, three, four.' "

District Attorney Ray Hamill was hounded by questions and complaints about why no arrest had been made. "The answer to the questions was that we didn't have enough evidence at the time to justify an arrest," Hamill would recall. "I was afraid we'd make an arrest, we'd get involved in a hearing prematurely, and the case would be dismissed. I felt we owed it to the community—and to Glenn's family—to make sure we had a case that would stick. I talked to Glenn's brothers and mother. They were cooperating with us."

Amid all the ferment, Glenn was buried in a local cemetery after a brief funeral service. A marble headstone later placed above the grave would bear this simple inscription: GLENN W. EVANS. AUGUST 14, 1966–JANUARY 28, 1987. MAY HE REST IN PEACE.

For the investigators trying to solve Glenn's murder, the opening stages of the investigation produced frustration after frustration. The investigators discovered, for example, that it would be fruitless to complete the neutron-activation test they had begun in an attempt to determine whether Travis Umstadter had fired a gun at about the time of the murder. After seizing Travis's .22-caliber revolver from his car, the officers found inside its cylinder four spent Remington cartridge cases and two unfired Remington bullets. But they knew that .22-caliber Remington ammunition did not contain the barium and antimony necessary to provide valid results in a neutron-activation test. Thus the test sample taken from Travis's hands was never sent to the state police crime lab for analysis.

Tests *were* completed, however, on two strands of hair found at the murder scene—one in Glenn Evans's hand, the other on the nearby table. The strands were compared under a microscope with the hair sample Travis had given the police. They did not match. A later examination showed the strands matched Glenn's own hair.

There also were tests on the floor mat seized from Travis's car. The mat showed no traces of gunpowder residue.

Fingerprints lifted from Glenn's apartment were either unidentifiable or too smudged to be useful as clues. One print lifted from a beer bottle in the apartment was perfect, but had been left by someone other than Travis or Glenn. The person's identity became a lingering mystery. As for Travis's gun, it yielded no fingerprints at all.

Still, the investigators persevered. State police ballistics expert Wayne Poust performed chemical tests on the paper towels discovered beneath the front seat of Travis's car. He detected a pattern of small nitrite spots characteristic of gunpowder residue.

More important, Poust ran a series of tests intended to determine whether Travis's gun was the murder weapon. He had in hand the revolver itself, the four spent cartridge cases, and the two unfired bullets found inside the gun's cylinder, plus the four bullets removed from Glenn's body—two of them mutilated.

Poust began by obtaining a batch of .22-caliber Remington ammunition similar to that found in Travis's gun. He then loaded the gun with test bullets from the new batch, fired several shots into a tank filled with water, and recovered the bullets from the tank.

Next, Poust set the test bullets one by one under a comparison microscope. Alongside each test bullet he placed one of the unmutilated bullets removed from Glenn's body. Peering into the microscope, Poust could see that the scratches left on the test bullets as they passed through the gun barrel—marks known as striations—lined up precisely with those on the bullets from the body. Only one gun could have left such perfectly matched striations on both sets of bullets.

Poust also conducted microscopic tests on the spent cartridge cases turned over to him by fellow investigators. He found that imperfections on the firing pin of Travis's gun matched the firing-pin impressions left on the spent cartridge cases.

Although the ballistics evidence seemed to demonstrate conclusively that Travis's gun had been the murder weapon, there still was no firm proof that Travis had fired the fatal shots. Poust's tests had succeeded only in placing Travis's gun inside Glenn Evans's apartment—not in placing Travis there. On the morning of the murder, the gun had lain for several hours in

Travis's Pontiac in the driveway of the Umstadter home before the police had assigned an officer to guard the car. Even a lawyer with minimal skills, much less a Lee Krause, could be expected to argue that anyone could have committed the murder and then dumped the gun in the car before it was placed under guard.

While the scientific evidence was being examined, investigator Herman Todd began questioning Travis's close friends— among them Dougie Smith, Tom Frisch, and Allan Rutledge. As it happened, Allan had been involved in a curious episode within days of the murder.

During the half-year since Kristen Umstadter's death, Allan had been trying to put behind him the piece of his life she had occupied. He had stowed in an out-of-the-way spot a box containing all his memorabilia from their romance—pictures of her, the letters she had written him, his class ring (which Kristen had kept until her death and Laraine had later returned to him). Allan had even sold the blue pickup truck he had driven on those long, romantic rides with Kristen. The truck stirred constant reminders too painful for him to bear. When he went looking for another truck, Allan deliberately avoided those with blue paint jobs. He bought a bright red model instead.

Still, no matter how great an effort he made, Allan discovered there was no putting Kristen out of his mind. All around him were memories of her. He told friends there was "not a minute" when Kristen was absent from his thoughts. He tried dating other girls, only to find himself comparing them with Kristen and deciding they did not measure up.

But it was a girl he had dated before going out with Kristen who precipitated the strange episode that followed Glenn Evans's murder. The girl was Jeanne Marie Coscia. By one of those quirks of small-town life, Allan had dated first Jeanne Marie and then Kristen, and Glenn had dated first Kristen and then Jeanne Marie.

Allan had not heard from Jeanne Marie for a long time. But then, two days after the murder, he received a phone call from her. Jeanne Marie never made clear why she was calling, but

Allan assumed she was trying to figure out all the circumstances surrounding the shooting. She did not mention her
phone conversation with Glenn on the night of the murder, and
Allan would not learn about it for months.

Yet, although that conversation had included Glenn's refer-
ences to Travis arriving at his apartment and looking "like he's
gonna kick my ass," Jeanne Marie actually accused *Allan* of
committing the murder. "She asked who could do such a
thing," Allan would recall. "I asked who wouldn't. Then she
accused me of doing it." Jeanne Marie would later say she
could not remember the conversation with Allan but would not
deny it had taken place. Allan's account left Herman Todd
with one more mystery to investigate. And Todd already was
fully occupied.

Early in the investigation, he was inundated with tips—
among them a report that Dougie Smith had been seen with
Travis on the night of the murder. When he questioned Dougie,
Todd recognized almost instantly that the young man represented a difficult challenge. If you wanted information from
Dougie, Todd discovered, you had to work for it—pulling it
from him syllable by syllable. He volunteered no wholesale revelations. Instead, he slipped a speck of information into the
conversation here and another speck there. Todd, a patient
man, decided to play Dougie's game. If Dougie wanted to
spend his time in session after session with the state police,
Todd would oblige him.

After the initial interview, Dougie went to see Travis and
asked what to do if questioned again. He said he did not want
to reveal anything that might hurt Travis.

"Just tell the truth," Travis told him.

Still, when Todd returned with more questions, Dougie remained cagy. It took several interviews before he mentioned
Travis's gun sliding out from beneath the car seat during their
ride. It took several more before he told of Travis's threat that
"Glenn won't live until spring." Dougie even held out information at least temporarily on seemingly minor incidents. He did
not mention until he had been questioned many times, for ex-

ample, that he and Travis had stopped at the Limerick bar during their ride to buy their third six-pack of beer.

Todd found Tom Frisch more forthcoming. Frisch obviously did not want to hurt Travis either, but nonetheless responded to Todd's questions with direct answers. He told of Travis calling Glenn an asshole and saying: "I'd like to kill the son of a bitch."

To the extent it was possible, Todd set out to reconstruct a chronology of Travis's movements on the day of the murder. He questioned Randy Young, who had driven Travis to work and back that day. Young recalled buying gasoline and making another brief stop after taking Travis home. Then, as he drove to his own home, he saw Travis turning his Pontiac off Highway 191 at the road leading to the new house the Umstadters were building near Lookout. Thus Todd could place Travis in northern Wayne County by late afternoon.

He also questioned Cord Meyer, Dave Pallis, Sherry Dennis, Clint Dennis, and others who had seen Travis at the Mountain View bar before and after he went cruising with Dougie Smith. On Travis's second visit, Clint Dennis recalled, he stayed until perhaps 12:15 A.M. Clint remembered watching Travis drive away about then.

Todd next made a test drive over the most direct route between the Mountain View and Glenn Evans's apartment. He chose a time when the weather and driving conditions approximated those on the night of the murder. Driving at fifty miles an hour, he arrived at the apartment in about twenty-one minutes.

Ray Hamill would come to regard Todd's chronology of the murder night as crucial, for, among other things, it lent credence to Jeanne Marie Coscia's story. Jeanne Marie had told the investigators she called Glenn at about midnight and talked to him for almost an hour before he suddenly blurted out word of Travis's arrival. That time sequence was entirely compatible with Clint Dennis's account and with the results of Todd's test drive.

Jeanne Marie's strange phone conversation with Allan Rutledge notwithstanding, Hamill and Todd believed her story of her talk with Glenn on the night of the murder. At the time Jeanne Marie first told the story to the police, the public had been given no information on what time the murder had been committed. "If she didn't have that conversation with Glenn, there's no way she'd have known what time to claim she talked to him," Hamill concluded.

Concurrently with investigating Travis Umstadter, Todd also was checking on the numerous others known to have harbored grudges against Glenn. Some had made outright threats against Glenn's life, others had merely muttered their resentment over Kristen Umstadter's death. Todd checked them all. Everyone except Travis seemed to have an alibi for the time of the murder.

Glenn's background also was subjected to intensive scrutiny. There always was the possibility that he had been murdered for reasons unrelated to Kristen's death. But Todd, Hamill, and the other investigators could discover no such reasons. "We really couldn't find anything very bad about Glenn aside from the accident case," Todd would recall. "He liked to drink. He was quite a party person. But that was about it. He didn't have an easy time of it growing up. He was pretty much on his own, so he partied a lot. But that wasn't surprising, considering he had no supervision."

Todd, in common with countless other law-enforcement officers, had been trained to concentrate on four key elements in investigating crimes: motive, means, capability, and opportunity. Travis Umstadter surely had a motive for killing Glenn Evans. He surely had the means, the .22-caliber revolver. As for capability, he knew how to fire the gun, but that answered only part of the question. Did Travis possess the mental and emotional capacity to kill another human being? That was a question mark. Opportunity remained a question mark as well. Travis was known to have been roaming around Wayne County on the night of the murder, but the investigators still were unable to put him inside Glenn's apartment.

There had been a time, as recently as six years earlier, when a

Wayne County district attorney would have asked a grand jury to make the final decision on what action was warranted in such a case. But Wayne, along with a group of other Pennsylvania counties, had abolished grand juries in 1981. The decision on how to proceed in a criminal case—no matter how flagrant—now rested solely with the DA. If he decided a prosecution was justified, he went into court and filed a written charge known as a criminal information that served as the equivalent of a grand jury's indictment.

Under constant public pressure for action in the case, Ray Hamill refused to be hurried. He waited three weeks while the investigators methodically pursued their evidence. But now, he knew, he must decide.

Hamill reviewed the case one more time with Herman Todd. Yes, there were gaps in the evidence—most notably the inability to put Travis Umstadter at the murder scene. But on the other side there was a substantial array of evidence implicating Travis.

Suspicion had been drawn to Travis at the outset not only by his family's role in reporting the shooting but also by his behavior immediately afterward and by the request that he be taken for a blood test. The murder weapon had been registered to the Umstadters and found in Travis's car. Various witnesses had told of hearing Travis voice threats against Glenn. And one witness—albeit a hearsay witness—had offered information purporting to place Travis at the scene shortly before the murder.

Altogether, Hamill concluded, it might be a largely circumstantial case, but it was a strong case nonetheless. He set to work on drawing up a criminal information:

The District Attorney of Wayne County by this information charges that between 12:30 A.M. and 3:30 A.M., January 28, 1987, at Route U.S. 6 and Township Route 472 in said County of Wayne, Travis Umstadter did commit criminal homicide, to wit: Murder of the first degree, in that he intentionally, knowingly, willfully and with malice aforethought, did cause the death of another human being, one Glenn Evans, all of which is against the Act of Assembly and the peace and dignity of the Commonwealth of Pennsylvania.

In addition to the first-degree murder count, the information charged Travis with lesser counts—third-degree murder and manslaughter. If a jury did not find the first-degree count warranted, it still could convict him on one of the lesser charges.

Under Pennsylvania law, first-degree murder carried a possible maximum sentence of death. Although there had not been an actual execution in Pennsylvania since 1962, almost a hundred convicted murderers were imprisoned in the state under death sentences. But Hamill had no intention of seeking the death penalty for Travis. From the evidence he had seen thus far, at least, the "aggravating circumstances" required for a death-penalty recommendation were just not there. Even so, if convicted of first-degree murder, Travis would still face a crushing sentence: a mandatory life term without the possibility of parole. If convicted on one of the lesser charges, he would be confronted by a sentence running from five to twenty years.

Laraine Umstadter had repeatedly told Lee Krause that, if the time ever came when charges were filed against Travis, she did not want him arrested at home. "I will not have him dragged out of the house in handcuffs," she said. "You tell us where and when you want us and we'll surrender him." Laraine especially wanted to avoid the spectacle of seeing Travis taken from the house in cuffs while camera crews videotaped the event for the evening news on the Scranton and Wilkes-Barre television stations.

Krause made advance arrangements with Ray Hamill to turn Travis in on demand. Hamill had initially feared Travis might try to flee while the case was under investigation. But now that Travis had stuck around this long, the DA saw minimal risk in permitting him to surrender.

When Hamill notified Krause that he was filing the criminal information, they agreed that Travis would surrender at the courthouse at 1:00 P.M. on Thursday, February 19. Laraine was infuriated, however, to find a television crew camped outside the Umstadter home when she, Travis, and Dave left for the courthouse. "Somebody had to tip those people off," she said.

More newspeople awaited them at the courthouse. Lee Krause also was there. Travis's face was expressionless as he climbed the courthouse steps. He was now sporting a thin mustache and a narrow, dark beard cut close to his chin and jaw. Stretched across his broad shoulders was a blue plaid shirt that hung outside his slacks.

Travis walked with a plodding, rolling gait through the lobby of the old courthouse. Herman Todd was waiting for him.

"I've got a warrant for your arrest," Todd said. Travis nodded.

He was then taken before Magistrate Bonnie Lewis for arraignment. Travis was formally presented with the charges against him. Bail was set at fifty thousand dollars, with a requirement that, if Travis went free on bail, he must continue to live with his parents.

While his parents tried to arrange bail, Travis was taken to the state police barracks for booking and then lodged temporarily in the Wayne County Prison—a small, white concrete structure next to the rear section of the courthouse. He was placed in a one-man cell measuring six-by-ten, with a bed, a steel sink, a steel toilet, a steel bookshelf, and an open metal cabinet for clothing. There were solid walls rather than bars on each side of the cell. The door, containing a small barred window, was made of solid steel. Another barred window looked out on the courthouse.

It was merely a cell in a county jail—a far cry from a hard-time state prison—but it gave Travis at least a taste of what might lie ahead. He'd had bigger thrills in his life.

Laraine and Dave arranged to bail him out by posting as collateral their nearly completed new home near Lookout. When Travis's release was approved, Joan Shaffer from the prothonotary's office walked over to the jail to bring him out.

Shaffer, a short, genial woman with a quick smile and an air of unflappability, had known both the Umstadter and Evans families for years. She had lived on the next property from the Evanses at one time and had seen Laraine Umstadter often around the courthouse. Shaffer liked both families but had noted disturbing changes in Laraine since Kristen's death: "Laraine's not the same woman she was before Kristen died. She's been obsessed with Kristen's death. She's not the only woman in Wayne County who ever lost a child in an automobile accident."

After Shaffer had presented the necessary paperwork to the jailers, they brought Travis from his cell. He and Shaffer made the short walk back to the courthouse in silence.

It was as if a great pall had descended over them. Shaffer recalls thinking: This is very sad. He's a nice kid. This whole thing is very sad.

TEN

One great fear haunted Ray Hamill during the six months that elapsed while he was preparing to prosecute Travis Umstadter. He could see it all happening in his mind's eye. The trial would reach a critical point. Then, out of the blue, Laraine or Dave Umstadter would take the witness stand and declare: "Travis didn't shoot Glenn Evans. I did."

Hamill would not believe such a confession. He didn't know if anyone else would, either. But he feared it just the same. "It could cause a lot of grief," Hamill told investigators working with him.

The DA already had grief enough—trying to figure out how to prepare his case. He didn't have the slightest idea what sort of defense Lee Krause planned to offer. Would Krause deny Travis had fired the fatal shots? Or would he concede that much and claim the shooting was somehow justified? If so, on what ground was it justified? Hamill did not have a clue. "Lee was doing a terrific job of keeping his people from talking before the trial," Hamill would recall.

Krause also was running the course on the entire range of trial preparation. He inundated the court with motions demanding information from Hamill on what the Commonwealth intended to prove. A motion for a bill of particulars demanded that Hamill "state specifically what words and/or deeds [of Travis's] constitute malice aforethought." A discovery motion demanded that Hamill reveal to Krause all statements, photographs, or other evidence he planned to introduce at the trial and all information dealing with "any relationship between the deceased, the accused, and any female subjects." Another motion sought the results of all the scientific tests conducted by the state police—among them those on Travis's gun, the bullets, the items checked for gunpowder residue, Travis's clothing, the hair samples, the fingerprints, and the blood sample taken from Travis's arm.

At the same time, Krause saw to it that Travis underwent extensive examination by two prominent Pennsylvania psychiatrists, Dr. John Lesniak of Scranton and Dr. Robert Sadoff of Jenkintown. But the results of those examinations, like much of Krause's evidence, would not be divulged until the trial.

Hamill, besides responding to Krause's demands, was methodically questioning his witnesses again and again—trying to ensure that he had not overlooked some seemingly trivial detail that might one day prove significant. He had already interviewed Frank Evans, one of Glenn's older brothers, several times but decided to talk to him once more before the trial. Frank Evans, twenty-three, worked at an underwear factory in Honesdale.

At one point during the interview, Hamill asked idly: "Was Glenn right-handed or left-handed?"

"He was left-handed," Evans said. "Why do you want to know?"

"I don't know why I want to know," Hamill replied. He truly did not know. It was simply another little piece of information to add to his profile of a murder victim.

The controversy that had enveloped the murder case from the start did not abate after Hamill filed charges against Travis. There were many in Wayne County who still were not satisfied. They argued that assuming Travis pulled the trigger, he was not the only one who should be held culpable.

"A lot of people in the community felt Laraine and Dave Umstadter drove Travis to murder," recalls one investigator assigned to the case. "They kept pressing him about Kristen's death. They just wouldn't let it go."

Joan Shaffer, among others, supports that view. "Everybody felt that Laraine and her husband pressed Travis—telling him he had to do something about all this," Shaffer says.

Sherry Dennis, the Mountain View bartender, says, "The

trouble with the Umstadters is that they think Kristen was perfect. And nobody's perfect."

Ray Hamill heard the talk about Laraine and Dave but did not consider it warranted. "We looked at every possibility of criminal liability," he says. "I don't think anyone ever suggested to Travis that he take Glenn Evans's life. We never considered prosecuting any other family members."

During the months of trial preparation, life unfolded as always in Wayne County—participants in the case and nonparticipants alike simply putting one day after another. The Umstadters moved out of the house on Erie Street, with all its tormenting memories of Kristen's death and Travis's troubles, into their now-completed home at Duck Harbor Pond.

Built on an eleven-acre tract thick with pines and hemlocks, the new house was a handsome, two-story wood structure measuring sixty-two by twenty-four. The ground floor had six rooms, plus a bathroom with a Jacuzzi. On the second floor—paneled in oak and knotty pine—there were two more rooms, another bath, and a walk-in attic above a two-car garage. There was a large wooden deck outside the house. Under other circumstances, the move into the new house might have represented a rebirth for the Umstadters. But they were not blessed with other circumstances.

Still, they tried to make the best of their predicament. Even in the face of the first-degree murder charge hanging over Travis, he and Chrissy Striffler continued discussing the possibility of marriage. The decision to marry might have been difficult for *any* young people. In this case, with the prospective bridegroom facing a potential life sentence in prison, the difficulty was substantially compounded.

But those who knew them well considered Travis and Chrissy deeply in love and totally committed to each other. Chrissy had not only stuck by Travis; she also had expressed firm belief in his innocence. And both of them seemed confident that when all the facts were heard, he would go free. Thus, after long and tortured conversations on what to do, they made their decision: They would go through with the wedding—murder case or no murder case.

Chrissy and Travis were married in a private ceremony on June 13, not quite two months before the scheduled start of the murder trial. The ceremony was so private, in fact, that even defense attorney Lee Krause did not learn about it until his client was already married. "It came as a surprise to me," Krause recalls.

It also came as a surprise to DA Ray Hamill. When Hamill heard about the marriage within days of the ceremony, the thought crossed his professionally suspicious mind that perhaps the wedding was somehow related to the murder case. After all, Pennsylvania was one of many states where a wife or husband could not be compelled to testify against a spouse. Hamill knew of no substantial evidence that Chrissy might be in a position to offer in the case. True, she had been with Travis in his car on the day when he had given Glenn Evans the finger on Main Street. But her testimony on the point was not essential to the Commonwealth's case; Hamill had another witness willing to describe the incident. On the other hand, who knew what sort of private revelations Travis might have made to Chrissy? Hamill recognized speculation on the point was idle. His hands were tied. There was nothing to do but try to content himself with the notion that, as he puts it, Travis and Chrissy "could have gotten married simply because they cared very much for each other."

The newlyweds moved into a mobile home parked on the property surrounding the Umstadter family's new house. That arrangement enabled Travis to establish a new home with his bride and still satisfy the bail requirement that he continue living with his parents.

Judge Robert Conway, who had presided over Glenn Evans's case, also would be on the bench for Travis's trial. Conway had ordered that the trial begin on Monday, August 3.

As the trial date neared, Honesdale found itself gripped by an atmosphere that might best be described as an admixture of curiosity, tension, and apprehension. The public wanted to know what had happened in the case and what *would* happen, but it was not crazy about paying the price of that curiosity in bad publicity and a tarnished community image.

America's news media are fond of labeling this murder case or that as "the trial of the century"—a term invariably overblown. But for Honesdale and Wayne County, the Travis Umstadter case would actually be the trial of the century and, in fact, the most celebrated trial in the community's history.

It seemed only fitting that such a case should summon as courtroom combatants two of Wayne County's more accomplished trial lawyers, Ray Hamill and Lee Krause. Although they offer contrasting styles and personalities, both are fiercely aggressive, quick-witted, solidly grounded in the law, and sharply attuned to community attitudes.

Hamill bears the look of an all-American boy grown into his midthirties without any significant erosion except for the salt and pepper in his hair. He is slim, with a firm mouth and jaw, a fair complexion, a quick smile, and the moves of an athlete. Besides playing amateur basketball, Hamill bowls competitively, takes part in other sports, and acts in local theatricals. He and his wife have a young son and daughter.

Born in Philadelphia, Hamill grew up in nearby Glenside, attended Dickinson College in Carlisle, and took his law degree from the University of Pittsburgh Law School in 1975. He then went to work as an attorney in Scranton for Northern Pennsylvania Legal Services, a government-funded agency providing legal help to low-income clients. When a vacancy occurred in the agency's Honesdale office, he transferred there in late 1976. By 1978 he had established a private practice in Honesdale.

Running as the Republican candidate, Hamill was elected district attorney in 1983. Four years later, he was reelected with bipartisan support.

Hamill projects an easy, open manner and a droll sense of humor. But he can turn tough in an instant—equally zealous in protecting the Commonwealth's interests and a defendant's constitutional rights. His open manner aside, he is an essentially cautious, conservative man who offers the appearance of measuring every word he utters.

Lee Krause is not so cautious—his language and courtroom behavior can be more extravagant than Hamill's—but at the same time his demeanor is less relaxed. He can be distant at times. His sense of humor is less apparent. Even on occasions when he appears to be relaxing—having a drink, say, at one of his favorite local bistros—his attitude reflects that his "on-duty" sign still is alight.

Krause was born in his family's apartment, above his father's pharmacy, in the Wayne County town of Waymart. He grew up just across the state line in Deposit, New York. "Some people consider me a transplant," Krause says, even though he is a Wayne County native and always has had prominent relatives in Honesdale (one uncle currently is president of the school board).

After graduation from Cornell University and Syracuse University Law School, Krause joined a Honesdale law firm and developed one of the busier practices in town. "Honesdale has been good to me," he says. "I've made a lot of money here." His lucrative practice permits him such indulgences as flying his Cessna regularly to vacation spots around the country—among them Hilton Head, South Carolina, where he owns a condominium. He also is an enthusiastic hunter. Like Hamill, he is married and has a son and daughter.

Krause is slightly built, with a dark complexion and dark hair. He is all lawyer and often expects laymen to think the way lawyers do. "You should never ask a question if you don't know the answer," he once cautioned a visitor. When the visitor pointed out that Krause had cited a lawyer's axiom that did not necessarily apply in other occupations, Krause seemed perplexed—as if the point had never dawned on him.

In addition to representing private clients, Krause handles the legal work of several branches of local government. He is, for instance, the attorney for the school district. He also is the county attorney, tending to all the county's legal affairs except the criminal cases that fall within Ray Hamill's province.

Thus, beyond all its other unusual circumstances, the Travis Umstadter murder trial would oblige the Wayne County attorney to square off in the courtroom against the Wayne County district attorney. That is not the sort of showdown that habitually arises in New York or Chicago or Houston or Los Angeles. But, still again, this was small-town America.

Preparing for the trial, Krause enjoyed one advantage over Hamill. He knew basically what the Commonwealth's case would be. Through the pretrial discovery process—designed to streamline trials and protect defendants' rights—Hamill turned over to Krause copies of witnesses' statements to the authorities, results of scientific tests, and other evidence critical to the Commonwealth case.

Hamill, for his part, remained in the dark on the strategy the defense would pursue. Shortly before the trial, Hamill drove with his wife and children to a beach house owned by his parents at Ocean City, New Jersey. They stayed for two weeks. Every day, Hamill walked alone along the beach for hours—looking out at the Atlantic, picking up an occasional shell, but primarily thinking his way through all the imponderables in the case.

"I tried to figure every possible defense and how I could counter it," Hamill would recall months later. "I didn't know, for example, whether Travis was going to take the stand. I also didn't know how some of our witnesses would react to being on the stand. We were dealing to a large extent with young people thrust into a tragic situation that affected this entire community. These were eighteen-, nineteen-, twenty-year-old kids being asked to testify against a friend. There was no telling how that would go. We live in a small community. Sometimes we don't realize how much our lives are intertwined."

Not long after Hamill's return from the Jersey shore, he would witness a graphic demonstration—in the courtroom—of just how small his community actually was and how closely its lives were intertwined. It would come at the very outset of Travis Umstadter's trial.

On the morning of August 3, Travis climbed the steps of the

courthouse—shoulders back, head erect, his body rolling slightly from side to side in what Lee Krause would call a "macho walk"—to confront the legal system empowered to lock him behind bars for the rest of his life. It was a roasting, muggy day, but a gentle breeze was drifting through the Poconos.

The handsome old courtroom in the original section of the courthouse was jammed with spectators, prospective jurors, lawyers, court personnel, and reporters. Laraine and Dave Umstadter were seated with Chrissy on a wooden bench in the spectators' section. Glenn Evans's brothers and their father, John Evans of Dalton, Pennsylvania, occupied another bench. Judge Conway was on the raised bench overlooking the courtroom in his black robe, Hamill and Krause at the counsel tables in their conservative gray lawyer suits.

Travis took his place at the defense table—still wearing his beard and mustache and, for this occasion, a fashionable beige sport jacket, contrasting brown slacks, a dress shirt, and a tie.

When Hamill and Krause began questioning prospective jurors, it became apparent that it would be impossible to find a jury in Wayne County unfamiliar with *this* case. Not only did everyone know about the case, almost everyone on the panel of prospective jurors knew someone involved in the case—the Umstadters, the Evanses, Hamill, Krause, the lawyers' associates, the investigators, or the witnesses.

Prospective juror Greg Olver testified that he was a frequent customer at the Umstadters' general store, that his sister had formerly dated Hamill's chief assistant, Mark Zimmer, and that he knew one of Krause's law partners. William Turana, Jr., said he worked in a bowling alley where Hamill bowled, that he knew Krause and the Umstadters, and that he was a good friend of Glenn Evans's brother Frank. Sandra Swensen's children had gone to school with the Umstadter children. Jacob Ripple's daughter had dated Dave Umstadter, Jr. Elizabeth Hopler knew both Krause and Hamill. Clayton Crum's attorney, Fred Howell, was Krause's partner. Crum also knew Hamill.

Amy Bayly went to school with Glenn. Randall Eldred belonged to a hunting club with Krause and knew the Umstadters. Patricia Watson testified that her husband worked at the Wayne County Ready Mix Company with Travis's friend Tom Frisch, listed as a prospective witness at the trial. Asked if she could put aside personal feelings and serve as an impartial juror, she replied: "I think I could."

Sally Finlan, a teacher, said Glenn Evans and his brothers had been among her students, that she knew their mother, and also was acquainted with Krause and Hamill. Roberta Conroy was one of Kristen Umstadter's teachers. Margaret Evanitsky went to school with Herman Todd. Michael Coar had lived next door to Todd. Lorraine Gallik lived down the street from Hamill and worked in a law office where she dealt not only with Hamill but also with Krause and Laraine Umstadter. Mark Tracy considered himself "a pretty good friend" of Travis's. Marcia Gager testified Krause was the attorney for her mother and brother. Susan Swingle worked for two years as Krause's legal secretary, knew Hamill, and bowled in a league with Frank Evans.

Here, in short, was incontrovertible evidence of just how tightly the lives of Wayne County residents were interlocked. In the face of such evidence, there was no pretense of finding a jury unfamiliar with Glenn Evans's murder or with those who figured to play central roles in Travis Umstadter's trial. There was no question, either, of moving the trial to another community. No motion for a change of venue had been filed. This case was Wayne County's business, and the consensus from the start had been that it should be decided in the Wayne County Courthouse by Wayne County jurors.

Thus the judge and the opposing lawyers were willing to make the accommodation of accepting jurors familiar with the case and the participants as long as those jurors gave evidence of being impartial. Krause asked many of them: "Based on everything you have either heard in the community or read or seen, can you honestly say to the court you have no fixed opinion of guilt or innocence?" Just as often, Hamill asked: "Is there any reason whatsoever that you know of why you could not sit as a fair and impartial juror in this case and render a verdict based upon the evidence that you are going to hear from that witness stand and the law as the court tells you the law to be?"

It took two and a half days, with the questioning of forty-two prospects, before twelve jurors and two alternates were chosen. The jury was seated just before the lunch recess on Wednesday, August 5.

Chosen as foreman was James Doherty, a retired insurance executive. The other members were Horace Davis, a retired truck driver; Elizabeth Hopler, selected even though she knew both lawyers and her husband was a former railroad police captain; Celin Cribbs, a nurse's aide; Theodore Porosky, a retired lumberman; Jane Parrish, a sewing-machine operator; Amy Bayly, employed by a nightwear manufacturer; Elsie Parry, a school bus driver; Patricia Watson, whose husband worked with Tom Frisch; Margaret Evanitsky, a secretary; Nancy Martone, a payroll clerk at a resort hotel; and Michael Coar, a shipping clerk with Moore Business Forms. The alternates were Timothy Jones, employed by an engineering firm, and John London, a retired airline maintenance manager.

Judge Conway, responding to repeated requests from Krause, agreed to sequester the jurors because of the seriousness of the case and the extensive news coverage. Each night during the trial, the jurors would be driven more than forty miles to the Best Western Motel in Port Jervis, New York, a Delaware River town where the Pennsylvania, New York, and New Jersey state lines intersect.

When court resumed after the lunch recess, Judge Conway told the jurors it had fallen to them "to perform one of the most solemn duties of citizenship—sitting in judgment on a criminal charge made by the Commonwealth against one of your fellow citizens." He gave them a detailed explanation of how they were expected to perform those duties and precisely how the trial would proceed. The judge told the jurors not to concern themselves with the possible penalty in case of a conviction—

that imposing sentence was his job, and that, in case any of them had scruples against capital punishment, the Commonwealth had decided not to seek a death sentence.

And then, without further preamble, the trial proper was suddenly under way. Ray Hamill was standing before the jury box and delivering his opening statement—his cool, unemotional tone of voice scarcely diminishing the power of his words:

"On January twenty-eighth, in the early-morning hours, Glenn Evans's life was taken from him not by an act of God, not by an accident, not by somebody's negligence or recklessness, but by four gunshot wounds to the head. He was shot in the eye. He was shot in the neck. And he was shot twice, ladies and gentlemen, behind his left ear. That is what took the life of Glenn Evans on January twenty-eighth."

Sketching an outline of his case, Hamill led the jurors chronologically through the events that would be described from the witness stand—from Lee Krause reporting a "possible shooting" to the discovery of Glenn's body to the gathering of evidence implicating Travis. "Now, ladies and gentlemen, it is never the Commonwealth's burden to show you a motive in any crime," Hamill told the jurors. "That is not a burden we bear. However, in this case we will present to you evidence of a motive through various witnesses."

After describing the circumstances of Kristen Umstadter's death, Hamill said: "We're going to produce witnesses who will tell you that in various forms at various times the defendant in this case expressed—let me just call it animosity—animosity toward Glenn Evans. He didn't think it was fair that his sister was dead and Glenn was alive. Glenn Evans stood trial on the charges brought against him on the basis of Kristen Umstadter's death. Glenn Evans was convicted the Wednesday before he died, before he was killed. Glenn Evans was awaiting sentence."

Hamill left it there—left it for the jurors to conclude that Travis had imposed his own sentence on Glenn.

Lee Krause, in his opening statement, said much of the evidence the Commonwealth would offer would go uncontested. But that did not mean he was conceding Travis was guilty of first-degree murder. Far from it, Krause told the jurors.

"This case is a tragedy," he said. "And I will show you through the testimony how this tragedy developed. This tragedy did not start on January twenty-seventh or twenty-eighth of this year. This tragedy started, ladies and gentlemen, on August sixteenth, 1986, with the death of Travis Umstadter's sister."

Krause said he would show that Travis and his family had gone through "sheer hell" over Kristen's death. "I will show you that the pressures imposed upon him by his family caused him to act in certain ways that would not be the normal ways to treat a death—any death in this society. I will show you the grief, the unnatural grief, that this family went through. I'm not condoning everything that happened in that family after August sixteenth, 1986. As a matter of fact, I blame a lot of it on that."

Laraine and Dave would take the stand, Krause said, to describe their unanswered questions about Kristen's death. "They'll testify that they continued to pressure Travis into finding out what happened," he told the jury. "Pressured him and asked questions that even today we don't know the answers to and never will. This pressure—this constant, constant pressure, grief over this loss—caused this gentleman to drink heavily, more heavily than he had in the past. And there will be evidence that he drank before this and he was underage. He did so many times."

Krause said his witnesses, as well as the Commonwealth's, would testify to Travis's animosity toward Glenn. "This animosity is something I believe you will understand as you see the tragedy unfold. The fabric of life of this family was ripped apart, torn, at that time."

Outlining for the jurors the defense Travis would offer, Krause said he would prove that Glenn was reckless and wild. "That he had continual beer parties in his apartment right up until the time of his death. That he was going to be evicted from that apartment within a few days. That he had little or no remorse. That he continued his life—his conduct after Travis's sister was killed—just as he had in the past, wild, carefree, drinking, excessive speed in his driving, and a disregard for human life."

Krause then offered a partial description of the night of the murder. "Ladies and gentlemen, keep in mind that at the time this happened Travis Umstadter had been drinking and depressed and upset," Krause said. "I will tell you that he went to Glenn Evans's home that night. That he went in that home and was asked to come in the home by Glenn Evans. And the reason that he was there was to find out the answers that his mother wanted—why did this happen, why, why did that girl get in this car with a drunk driver?"

Ray Hamill did not quite shout: "Bingo!" But he would later recall that he was thinking it—or, at least, its courtroom equivalent. All those months, Hamill had worried about the big hole in his case: his inability to place Travis inside Glenn's apartment. And now, at the very outset of the trial, Krause had voluntarily plugged the hole for him.

It was not, by any means, a blunder on Krause's part. On the contrary, conceding Travis's presence in the apartment was a calculated piece of strategy essential to the defense Krause had painstakingly devised. He had kept Hamill guessing for a half-year on what that strategy would be, but there was no percentage in being coy at this stage of the case.

There were three main elements to the strategy Krause had chosen. One was self-defense—a claim that Glenn had attacked Travis that night in the apartment. The second was an appeal for the jury to consider the passions in play that night—a plea admittedly directed at the emotions rather than the law. The third was a defense of diminished capacity—a claim, based on psychiatric evidence, that Travis's drinking that night had deprived him of the ability to form a specific intent to commit premeditated murder.

"You will hear from psychiatrists who have examined Mr. Umstadter that he had a diminished capacity at the time of this shooting," Krause told the jurors. "This does not absolve him, the court will tell you, of all guilt. You can use that evidence to reduce the crime of first-degree murder to a lesser crime."

But Krause was not inviting a conviction on *any* count, merely using that as a fallback position. "Keep in mind I do not have to prove innocence," he said. "Nor do I have to prove anything beyond a reasonable doubt. The Commonwealth must prove it. Keep in mind that I am not calling this a murder case. I'm calling it a tragedy case. I'm not looking for sympathy in this case. I'm going to show you a tragic set of facts. After you have heard all the testimony, I believe that you will have a duty to acquit Mr. Umstadter of all of the charges and not compound that tragedy."

Judge Conway turned to Ray Hamill. "Call your first witness," he said.

"The Commonwealth calls Trooper Robert Fuehrer, Your Honor," Hamill replied.

Bob Fuehrer made a perfect opening witness—solid, avuncular, the sort of man inclined to inspire confidence in a jury. He testified that he and Trooper Andrew Piezga were writing reports in the state police barracks at about 3:30 A.M. on January 28 when the call came in from Lee Krause reporting a "possible shooting." Fuehrer described going with Piezga to meet Krause at the Umstadter home after initial confusion over how to find the place.

He said the Umstadters were in the kitchen when he and Piezga arrived. "The defendant had his head down and seemed to be crying," he said. "I read the rights to the general area, but I concentrated on the defendant."

"Was anything said by attorney Krause at that time?" Hamill asked.

"At that time he asked me if his client could go for a blood test," Fuehrer replied. He said he assigned Piezga to take Travis to the hospital for the test.

Here, at the very outset of the trial, Hamill began trying to knock down Krause's diminished-capacity defense. "Trooper, how long did you have the occasion to view the defendant's behavior and actions while you were in that home that night?" he asked.

"A very short period," Fuehrer said. "I'm going to say at the very most five minutes."

"In the course of the five minutes that you observed his conduct, what, if anything, out of the usual did you observe?"

"Nothing out of the usual, sir, except that he was crying and seemed to be remorsed."

"He didn't have any trouble with his speech?"

"No, sir, he did not."

"His reactions were appropriate?"

"Objection!" Krause said. "I don't know what appropriate means."

"Sustained," the judge ruled.

"When you asked him a question, did he respond?" Hamill asked.

"When I asked him questions, he did respond," Fuehrer said. He told of asking Travis his name, his date of birth, and how to spell "Umstadter"—all of which Travis answered correctly.

Fuehrer described driving to Glenn Evans's apartment with Krause while Piezga took Travis to the hospital for the blood test. At the apartment, he said, he looked inside through a pane of glass in the door.

Q. What did you observe?
A. I observed a body underneath the table.
Q. Did you go into the apartment?
A. Yes, I did, sir.
Q. Did attorney Krause go in with you?
A. Yes, he did. The door was unlocked.
Q. What, if anything, did you do?
A. I went over to check the body to see what I had— whether he was wounded or, as it turned out, he was dead.
Q. What were you able to observe when you went over to the body of Glenn Evans?
A. His eyes were partially open and there was some black over the top of his left eye. And, when I checked his

carotid artery, there was a hole at the left side of the carotid artery around the neck area.

Later, Fuehrer said, he discovered two more bullet holes behind Glenn's left ear. He told of searching the apartment, of coming upon Mark Evans asleep upstairs, and of calling in other investigators and support personnel. When Herman Todd arrived to take over the investigation, Fuehrer immediately informed him that no weapon had yet been found. "Attorney Krause said, in essence, if you look in the vehicle owned by Travis Umstadter you might find the weapon," Fuehrer testified.

"Did he indicate where the vehicle was located?" Hamill asked.

"Yes, sir, he did. In front of the Umstadter home."

On cross-examination, Lee Krause emphasized the cooperation he had provided on behalf of the Umstadters from the beginning of the investigation. "Officer, throughout our conversations that evening, isn't it true that I cooperated with everything you asked me to do?" he asked.

"One hundred percent," Fuehrer replied.

Trooper Piezga was called as the next witness. He told of receiving the original call from Krause at the barracks, then accompanying Fuehrer to the Umstadter home and taking Travis to the hospital for the blood test. In questioning Piezga, Hamill again sought to undermine the diminished-capacity defense.

"While you were at the Umstadter home, did the defendant display any difficulty of any kind with his motor skills?" Hamill asked.

"No, he didn't," Piezga replied.

"He sat properly?"

"Yes."

"He was able to walk properly?"

"Yes."

"When he was asked a question, he responded?"

"Yes."

Piezga said Travis had no trouble sitting upright during the ride to the hospital—even when the car turned sharp corners—and that he scrupulously followed the instructions of the lab technician who drew his blood. The trooper testified he later took Travis to the state police barracks and spent another hour and a half with him. During all that time, Piezga said, he saw no indication that Travis was having trouble with his motor skills, speech, or other faculties. Piezga left the barracks at about 6:30 A.M. to relieve another officer guarding Travis's Pontiac in the driveway of the Umstadter home.

"Did you have occasion while you were observing that vehicle to notice how it was parked?" Hamill asked.

"Yes," Piezga said. "The car was parked facing a retaining wall that was alongside of the house, with the rear of the vehicle perpendicular to the roadway."

"Was there anything unusual at all about the way it was parked?"

"No."

It was a point Hamill would make repeatedly during the trial: If Travis was so drunk the night of the shooting that his capacity to function was diminished, how come he could park his car perfectly in a tight space and perform other complex acts?

When Lee Krause cross-examined Piezga, he challenged the testimony that Travis showed no obvious indications of heavy drinking. "Did you ask Travis to take any field sobriety test for you or anything of that nature?" Krause asked.

"No," Piezga answered.

"Officer, were you present when I told my client not to make any statements until I had an opportunity to talk to him?"

"Yes."

"What statements did he make to you after I told him not to say anything?"

"He didn't make any statements to myself."

"Well, then, how do you know that he spoke clearly?"

"He spoke to his father. His father asked him what he did

that day. There was a conversation relative to he was working on a house that day."

Piezga was followed to the stand by Wayne Poust, the state police ballistics expert who conducted the tests on Travis's .22-caliber revolver. Hamill explained to the jurors that Poust was testifying out of order. Ordinarily he would not have been called until the proper foundation had been established with testimony, for example, on the seizure of the gun and the recovery of bullets from Glenn Evans's body. But since Poust was in constant demand to testify in cases throughout Pennsylvania, it was agreed that his appearance at Travis's trial would be timed to accommodate his travel schedule. Poust, a supervisor in the state police ballistics section, testified he had worked there for twelve years and had received advanced ballistics training from the FBI and other federal agencies. With Krause's concurrence, he was accepted as an expert witness.

Poust told of matching two of the bullets recovered from Glenn's body to Travis's revolver. The other two recovered bullets were too mutilated to be matched to any specific gun, he said. He testified the four spent cartridge cases recovered by the police bore marks that matched test impressions made by the firing pin on Travis's gun.

In addition, Poust said, he performed a series of other tests on the gun. "My examination showed it to be functional and capable of discharging ammunition," he testified.

"I did shock and drop tests. The weapon was dropped from various heights. I also tapped it in various locations around the sides of the weapon with a nylon-tipped hammer to see if I could induce the weapon to discharge. In those tests, I could not induce it to discharge by dropping it and striking a blow." Poust also conducted tests determining that it took three pounds, eight ounces of pressure on the trigger to fire the gun. Simply put, Travis's gun had not likely been fired by accident—especially not four times.

Using photographs of powder burns surrounding two bullet wounds on Glenn's body, Poust also conducted tests intended to determine how close the gun had been to Glenn when fired. "I did powder-pattern tests with the weapon by firing test patterns with the same type of ammunition that was submitted and at various distances. I then compared them with powder patterns on the photographs. Among the photographs I had received, I saw powder patterns on two wounds—one around the area of the left eye and the other around the lower hole below the left ear. By comparing the test powder patterns with those appearing on the photographs, I was able to determine that those two shots had been fired from a distance of greater than six inches and less than twenty-four inches."

Poust then described performing a chemical test for gunpowder residue on the paper towels seized from Travis's car. "Nitrite is a product of the burning of gunpowder," he testified. "I did find nitrite present on one of the paper towels."

Now Hamill got down to placing on the record a crucial element of his case—just how Travis's revolver worked and how those mechanics might offer a clue to the killer's intent. "Would you explain to the jury, please, how that weapon operates?" Hamill asked.

"This is a single-action weapon," Poust replied. "To fire the weapon you pull the hammer all the way back as far as it goes, make sure the weapon is straight, and fire. You pull the trigger. To fire the next shot you must pull the hammer all the way back again and then pull the trigger. And for each successive shot it requires that you manually pull the hammer back again, then pull the trigger."

It seemed, in short, not the ideal weapon for a crime of passion.

Lee Krause launched his cross-examination with a challenge to the validity of Poust's nitrite test for gunpowder residue. Wasn't it true that nitrites were present in numerous places in the environment? "There are even nitrites in urine, aren't there?" Krause asked.

"There may be," Poust said. "I don't know."

"There is a whole host of chemicals or products that are

common, everyday chemicals or products, are there not?" the defense lawyer asked.

"There are other nitrites in dyes," Poust replied. "There are other nitrites in meat preservatives."

"There are nitrites in inks, aren't there?"

"There very well may be."

Krause had made a seemingly insignificant point. It contributed almost nothing to the success of his overall defense strategy. But he was giving Hamill no free rides.

"Now, calling your attention to the gun itself," Krause told Poust, "you indicate it has, I believe, three pounds, eight ounces of pressure needed to pull the trigger. Is that correct?"

"That is correct."

"And is that normal for this type of weapon?"

"I'd say it was within the general range."

"To apply that amount of pressure is not something that you need two hands to do. It's something you could do with a single hand, is that correct, with one finger?"

"That's correct."

Hamill called as his next witness state police identification expert John Fox, a trooper for more than twenty years. Fox testified he had been called out of bed in the early-morning hours on January 28 to work on the Glenn Evans case. He went to Glenn's apartment, photographed the murder scene, took fingerprints, and performed several tests.

When Hamill tried to place Fox's photographs in evidence, Krause objected strenuously to the introduction of one picture. It showed Glenn's body after it had been moved from the spot where it had originally been found. A cigarette, partly smeared with blood, had been found beneath the body and was visible in the photograph. Hamill would contend throughout the trial that Glenn apparently had been smoking the cigarette when shot. He used that contention to try to undercut Krause's self-defense theory—arguing that it would have been unlikely for Glenn to keep a cigarette in his mouth while carrying out a supposed attack on Travis. Krause contended there were numerous other possible explanations for the cigarette's presence beneath the body. He also argued that the picture was inflammatory because of the blood on the cigarette and would confuse the jury because it did not accurately depict the body's position when discovered.

But the judge said he saw no reason to bar the picture as long as the jury was informed the body had been moved. "It's a colored photograph that simply shows the blood stains and some blood on the back of the victim," Conway said. "I don't see it as that inflammatory. Objection overruled."

Under Hamill's questioning, trooper Fox identified and described numerous pictures he had taken at Glenn's apartment. He also told of conducting preliminary neutron-activation tests on the hands of both Travis and Glenn in an attempt to determine whether either of them had recently fired a gun. But he explained that the tests were not completed because the type of ammunition in Travis's gun did not contain the barium and antimony necessary for valid results.

Fox testified that he examined Glenn's apartment for signs of forced entry but found none. Hamill then asked him if he had found any fingerprints. Fox said he had lifted two partial fingerprints from a beer bottle found on the edge of the table in Glenn's apartment. He said he compared them with inked photographs taken from Travis and from Glenn's body, but they did not match. Nor did they match any other known prints.

"Did you obtain fingerprints off any other items in the apartment?" Hamill asked.

"No, sir. The other items that I did process for latent fingerprints were all smudged."

"Officer, did you check the revolver for fingerprints?"

"Yes, sir, I did."

"Were you able to obtain any fingerprints from that revolver?"

"No, sir."

In cross-examining Fox, Krause asked: "Could you ascertain from your observations of the crime scene what position the body was in when the victim was shot?"

"In my opinion, based on the location of the blood on the

kitchen table, based on the location of the blood on the victim's arms, I believe at the time that he was on the west side of the kitchen table when he was shot—either in a sitting or standing position," Fox said.

"Either in a sitting or standing position?"

"Yes, sir."

Q. Did you find any fingerprints of the defendant, Mr. Umstadter, on that table?

A. I didn't find any prints.

Q. Did you notice in your chemical analysis or dusting any attempt to wipe clean the surface area of the table?

A. No, sir.

Q. Did you notice any attempt to wipe clean the weapon or any other exhibits?

A. No, sir.

Q. In other words, those exhibits would be consistent with having smudges on them but no attempt to hide or cover up?

A. That's correct.

The defense lawyer then questioned Fox about a pair of scissors found among other items on the table in Glenn's apartment. "Did you examine these scissors for fingerprints?" he asked.

"Yes, I did," Fox said.

"Did you find any?"

"No, sir, I did not. Smudges."

"Now, smudges are what?"

"Smudges are usually created when an item is touched and basically there is too much pressure applied. A rubbing effect will cause a smudge, too."

"So, in other words, a great deal of pressure applied to these scissors would leave a smudge, would it not?"

"Yes, sir."

Called as the first nonpolice witness in the trial was Jack Rickert, who lived next door to Glenn Evans and heard the murder being committed but did not initially recognize the sounds for what they were. Under Hamill's questioning, Rickert testified that he went to bed just after ten o'clock on the night of January 27. Between ten and midnight, he said, he heard noises four or five times from the Evans apartment—the door slamming, people running up and down the stairs, loud voices as if a party might have been in progress. Once or twice, he heard cars leaving the parking lot. Still, he managed to fall asleep—only to be disturbed later by more noise from the Evans apartment.

"At approximately two to two-thirty A.M., I was awakened by banging noises—almost as if someone had banged on the wall—and then that was followed by a thump," Rickert testified. "It sounded like someone had fallen or a piece of furniture had fallen onto the floor."

"Did you hear anything other than the bangs and then a thump?" Ray Hamill asked.

"Yes. Then the front door slammed and a few seconds later a car left the parking lot."

Q. How do you know it was the front door of the Evans apartment that slammed shut?

A. I heard it many times before. The door was tough to shut and, every time you shut it, you had to slam it. And, as you slammed it, it would shake the walls of our apartment.

Q. You say you heard a car take off. Would you tell the ladies and gentlemen of the jury specifically what you heard in that regard?

A. As the car left, it appeared to leave in a hurry. It spun gravel up either on the side of the building or on a car, I'm not sure which.

Under Krause's cross-examination, Rickert testified that he frequently complained about loud parties and other noise from the Evans apartment. "Did you see individuals coming in and out of that apartment with beer or intoxicants?" Krause asked.

"I may have seen beer half a dozen times, yes," Rickert said.

Krause asked if Rickert saw anyone carrying beer into or out of the Evans apartment on the night of the murder. "That night, no," Rickert replied. "I didn't see anyone enter or leave that night."

"Okay. And you didn't see Mr. Umstadter enter or leave, did you?"

"No, I did not."

"Now, as you described to the jury the bangs that you heard on the night of the twenty-seventh, early-morning hours of the twenty-eighth, would you say this noise all occurred within about four seconds?"

"No. No, it was longer than that."

"Okay. Immediately after the noise and the thump, you heard the door slam shut, is that right?"

"That was within a few seconds, yes."

During a recess following Rickert's testimony, the lawyers joined Judge Conway in his chambers for a discussion of a problem that had arisen—a problem with overtones of black humor. County coroner Young W. Lee was to be the next witness. Hamill had wanted Lee to use a plastic model of a human skull during his testimony, so he could point out the nature of Glenn's bullet wounds and the bullets' apparent trajectories.

The trouble was that the model kept falling apart. Hamill understandably did not want to put Lee on the stand with a skull falling to pieces. "I asked Dr. Lee if he could obtain another authentic illustration of the human skull," Hamill told the judge. "Sure enough, he has. Now, it is nothing remarkable. It's a human skull used for teaching purposes at the hospital and the like."

Hamill, who had carried the skull into the judge's chambers but kept it covered, now unveiled it for inspection.

"It's a plastic model?" Judge Conway asked.

"No, it's a human skull."

Hamill explained that the top of the skull was removable, so a viewer could look inside it. Lee had marked points on the skull to indicate where bullets had entered Glenn's head and where they had lodged.

"Let me see that," the judge said. After examining the skull, he still found it hard to believe it was the genuine article. "So this is not plastic?" he asked. "It is a human skull?"

"That is what Dr. Lee told me," Hamill replied.

"That doesn't look any different to me," Conway said. "But I'll take his word for it."

Krause objected to permitting introduction of the skull as an exhibit in the trial. He argued that Hamill had been obliged to make all prospective exhibits available to him before the trial—during the discovery process—so he could prepare his defense and challenge any improper evidence. "This is the first time I've seen this," Krause said. He also contended that the sight of the skull "can be shocking and inflammatory to the jury."

The judge, however, disagreed. "I can't tell the difference whether it's a plastic or human skull," he said. "It's simply a yellow-looking skull. And, for that reason, objection overruled."

It was not one of the great victories in the history of American jurisprudence. But a relieved Ray Hamill considered it a triumph nonetheless.

ELEVEN

The skull was marked as Commonwealth's Exhibit Eleven but was nowhere in sight when county coroner Young W. Lee took the stand. Dr. Lee—short, slightly built, a man of precise movements and spare animation—did not need any props at the outset of his testimony.

He ran through his medical credentials and was accepted as an expert witness. Under Ray Hamill's questioning, Lee testified that his autopsy on Glenn Evans's body revealed the four bullet wounds and substantial bleeding around those wounds but no other injuries. He said the wound over Glenn's left eye and one wound behind the left ear bore significant powder burns, that the second wound behind the ear had fewer powder burns, and that the neck wound had none.

"Did the internal examination reveal anything to you as far as the course of these bullets?" Hamill asked.

"Yes," Lee said. "They had skull fractures and penetrating gunshot wounds over the brain and penetrating gunshot wounds of the brain stems."

Lee spoke in a sort of shorthand—a compound of his medical training and his Chinese roots. It took an effort, at times, to follow his testimony. But Hamill plunged ahead.

"Now, the brain stems, Doctor, if I'm not mistaken, are at the base of our brain?"

"Yes," Lee said. "This brain stem has vital part of the nerve system. Very important. Life-controlling system within the brain stems."

Now Hamill brought out the skull. He handed it to Lee and asked whether the coroner had used it as a teaching aid for medical students and other doctors.

"Yes," Lee said. "I have used this one for about thirty-five years."

Holding the skull, Lee pointed out the trajectory of each bullet fired into Glenn's body—identified for purposes of his testimony as Bullets A, B, C, and D. He demonstrated where each bullet entered Glenn's head, where it traveled, and where it finally lodged.

"So, if I may summarize, Bullet A entered above the eye, passed through the brain, and embedded in the back of the skull?" Hamill asked.

"Yes," Lee replied.

Q. Bullet B entered in the neck and went up and came to rest in the brain-stem area?

A. Past the brain stem.

Q. And Bullet C again went through the brain stem?

A. Yes.

Q. And Bullet D was distorted and fragmented?

A. Yes.

Q. Doctor, in your professional opinion, how many of these bullet wounds were fatal shots?

A. Based on my medical knowledge, all four gunshot wounds passed through the vital portion of the brain. So I would say four wounds are all fatal wounds.

Q. Each wound is fatal?

A. Yes.

Q. How quickly would death occur with the shots?

A. I cannot define any exact time. However, brain stem controls our life. In case bullet pass through the brain stem, we usually call—unscientific terms—we call instant killing, instant dying. So possibly a few seconds to die.

Q. Doctor, do you have an opinion to a reasonable degree of medical certainty as to the cause of death of Glenn Evans?

A. Yes, the cause of death of Glenn Evans is the penetrating gunshot wound to the brain and brain stem.

Hamill then questioned Lee about his examination of the body when called to Glenn's apartment in the early-morning hours. After confirming that Glenn was indeed dead, Lee said, he tried to determine the time of death.

"What procedure do you follow, Doctor?" Hamill asked.

"First, we check the body for the loss of body temperature," Lee said. "And, number two, we can find out the lividity, the discoloration of skin. Usually, if somebody die and lay down, it develops some purple colors. And the next factor is rigor mortis—the stiffness of body. We also have circumstantial factors, such as bleeding, to check. So this case I found a large amount of blood around the head. So I used the blood findings to help determine estimated time of death."

"Okay, Doctor, would you tell us, please, do you have an opinion within a reasonable degree of medical certainty as to time of death?"

"Yes, based on these four factors, my most precise medical certainty is around two A.M. to three A.M."

On cross-examination, Krause tried to counter one of the more damaging elements in the case against Travis—the evidence that two of the gunshots had been fired into the *back* of Glenn's head. If Krause were to pursue the self-defense claim mentioned in his opening statement to the jury, it might be difficult to explain away the shots fired from the rear.

Krause began by asking whether Lee could tell which bullet wound had been inflicted first. The coroner replied that bleeding patterns indicated the shot above the left eye could have been the first. Krause then wanted to know whether the first shot—assuming it struck Glenn from the front—would have caused him to turn his head. "Would that be a natural reaction?" he asked.

But Lee's response offered the defense little help. The coroner said that under the circumstances Krause had described, the victim's head would normally snap backward and then bounce forward again. "I don't know which way it would fall," he said. "I can't answer that."

Krause then asked whether Lee had noticed blood on the table in Glenn's apartment. "Yes," Lee replied.

"Would that lead you to believe, Doctor, that at the time of the shooting the victim was either seated or could have been standing above the table?"

"Well, to the best of my knowledge, looks like the victim was sitting on the chair."

"Could the victim have been rising from the chair?"

"I can't answer that. I do not know."

When Lee left the stand, Hamill began presenting testimony intended to track Travis's movements during the day and night leading to the murder. The testimony also was intended to combat the defense contention that Travis was so drunk on the night of the murder he was incapable of forming the criminal intent necessary to sustain the most serious charges against him.

Randy Young, who worked with Travis and had driven him to and from their job site on the day preceding the killing, testified he ran into Travis that night in the Mountain View bar. He said Travis gave no indication he was drunk.

Clint Dennis, working as the Mountain View's bartender at the time, concurred. He testified Travis had no trouble speaking, walking, or operating the jukebox.

Next, Hamill called one of his more important witnesses— Dougie Smith. The cagy game Dougie had played with Herman Todd and other investigators during earlier stages of the case was now over. By this point, he seemed to be cooperating fully with the authorities—too fully, as it turned out, for Travis's taste.

Dougie testified he considered Travis a close friend. In fact, he said, Travis had actually lived with him for seven months during 1985 while Dougie's parents were temporarily away from home. He described the ride he and Travis had taken all over Wayne County, drinking beer after beer, on the night of the shooting. Dougie told how Travis's gun had slid out from beneath the car seat, how Travis had placed it on the seat, and it had then tumbled to the floor—in each case because the brakes had suddenly been applied.

Ray Hamill showed Dougie the revolver identified as the murder weapon. "To the best of your recollection and belief, is that the gun and holster that was in the car that night?" he asked.

"Yes," Dougie said.

"Now, Doug, had you seen that gun and holster before that night?"

"Yes. Lots."

"How is it that you recognize that as being the gun and holster?"

"Got gold on it."

"Did the defendant ever tell you how he got that gun?"

"Yes. His father gave it to him for Christmas."

Hamill then asked if Dougie had seen Travis on the Saturday night before the shooting. Dougie said he had—at the bar called Cheers across the state line in Cochecton.

> Q. How long did you see him that night?
> A. Three or four hours.
> Q. Doug, did you have any conversation with the defendant about his sister's death?
> A. Yes.
> Q. Would you tell the ladies and gentlemen of the jury, please, what the defendant said to you that evening?
> A. He said he missed her.
> Q. Did he say anything else to you?
> A. He was going to get even.
> Q. Anything else?
> A. And that Glenn wouldn't live until spring.

"No further questions," Hamill said. He knew that last sentence of Dougie's was perhaps the most damaging line of testimony yet delivered against Travis. It was the perfect place to stop. But what impression Dougie's last line had made on the jurors was hard to judge. Both Hamill and Krause were watching the jury box at the time. Neither detected a flicker of expression on any juror's face.

Krause, nonetheless, recognized that the full range of Dougie's testimony posed a serious threat to the defense case. He launched an aggressive cross-examination intended to undercut that testimony. During Dougie's direct testimony describing his long ride with Travis, he had said each of them drank about five beers. But Krause drew from Dougie the information that there were three six-packs in the car at one time or another, plus three loose bottles.

"How many beers were left in the car when Travis dropped you off?" Krause asked.

"Three," Dougie said.

"Okay. I'm not very good at math, but let's try to work this out. It was three six-packs—that is eighteen beers—and three more is twenty-one. There were three beers left when you were done. So we got eighteen bottles or cans of beer that were consumed while you and he drove around. Wouldn't that be a more accurate statement than what you just told the jury?"

"Yes."

"Did you drink beer for beer? About equal?"

"Yes."

"So now we're up to about equal. We had about nine each, didn't we?"

"Yep."

"Almost doubling what you just told the jury you had, right?"

"Right."

"Okay. Toward the end he slurred his speech a little bit, is that right?"

"Right."

Krause questioned Dougie about the incident during the ride in which Travis had gotten his car stuck in the snow on an unplowed section of the parking area at Lake Wallenpaupack. Dougie said he doubted Travis would have driven through the snow if he had not been drinking. He testified that Travis had been drinking "considerably more" since Kristen's death.

Q. Did you and Travis talk about the death of his sister?

A. Sometimes.

Q. That upset him?

A. A little.

Q. Isn't it true, Doug, that on some occasions when you talked about his sister that even you would mention Glenn Evans didn't get enough and even you would like to get Glenn Evans?

A. Yes.

Q. Didn't you, on some of these occasions when you and Travis were out drinking, didn't you say if you could get him you would?

A. Yes.

Q. Do you remember other people, other friends that were with you and Travis, saying the same thing?

A. Uh-huh, yes.

Q. That they'd like to get Glenn Evans and he didn't get enough?

A. Right.

Q. When he said that statement to you, that he wouldn't live until spring, did you feel that he was going to go out and kill him?

A. No.

Q. That is something you all said, isn't it?

A. Uh-huh, yes.

When Ray Hamill got another crack at questioning Dougie, he returned to the barroom conversation. "Doug, on the Saturday night that Travis talked to you, Mr. Krause has brought up the discussion that the punishment wasn't enough," Hamill said. "Was there a discussion as far as the punishment that Glenn Evans was to receive?"

"Five years or ten-thousand-dollar fine," Dougie said.

"And that was as a result of a trial that Glenn Evans had the Wednesday before that Saturday night, isn't it?"

"Yes."

"So that's a total of four days between the point in time that

Glenn Evans had been convicted and the time that this conversation with the defendant took place?"

"Yes."

"Thank you," Hamill said. Dougie stepped down from the stand. He did not know it at that moment, but his friendship with Travis was over. After hearing Dougie's testimony, Travis would not talk to him again.

The next witness was Herman Todd, who had directed the state police investigation of the Evans murder. Todd cut an imposing figure—a big, handsome man who looked as if he could arm-wrestle a bear.

Hamill's questioning carried Todd through his entire investigation of the case, from the moment he took charge at the murder scene through such other events as seizing the gun from Travis's car and trying to question Travis at the state police barracks. While at the barracks, Todd said, Travis agreed to turn over to the police the clothes he had been wearing.

"Did the defendant say anything to you during the time that he was handing you his apparel?" Hamill asked.

"Yes," Todd said. "Before he handed me anything, he referred to an outer shirt he had and was handing to me. He said, 'Do you want this? I wasn't wearing it at the time.'"

On cross-examination, Krause drew from Todd a concession that the defense had cooperated fully during the police investigation—permitting the search of Travis's automobile, providing hair samples, fingerprints, the clothing, and other items of evidence.

"There has been no indication that Travis Umstadter's fingerprints are on the gun, isn't that right?" Krause asked.

"That's right," Todd answered.

"There is no indication that any of the clothes he had on had blood on it, is that right?"

"That's correct."

"There is no indication of any of the tests, as a matter of fact, placing Travis Umstadter at the scene of this crime, isn't that right?"

"That's correct, yes."

Hamill next called Tom Frisch to the stand to testify about his friendship with Travis and antagonistic remarks he had heard Travis make toward Glenn Evans. Frisch said he talked often with Travis about Kristen's death. The first such conversation, he said, occurred only a day after Kristen was killed. Asked if Travis said anything about Glenn, Frisch replied: "He called him a fuckin' asshole and said he should pay for what he did to his sister."

Hamill asked what Travis said in subsequent conversations. "That Glenn was an asshole and he should have died," Frisch responded. "He'd like to kill the son of a bitch. His sister's dead now and Glenn's still alive and he should pay." Frisch said several of their friends felt the same way Travis did.

"How about yourself?" Hamill asked. "Did you ever tell Travis that you, yourself, would like to see some harm come to Glenn Evans?"

"Yes," Frisch said.

"Why did you say such a thing?"

"Because I loved Kristen Umstadter just like Travis did. She was a real close friend of mine. I just didn't figure what happened in the accident was right."

When Krause took over on cross-examination, he asked Frisch to describe the relationship between Travis and Kristen. "He had more feelings toward his sister than anyone I ever saw," Frisch replied. "More feelings toward his sister than I do even toward my own—and I figure I have a pretty close relationship with my sisters."

"Now, when you had these conversations with Travis and statements were made by Travis that he'd like to kill Glenn or whatever, you said these same things, too, didn't you?" Krause asked.

"Yes," Frisch said.

"Did you ever intend them to mean that you were actually going to go out and kill him?"

"No. Just a figure of speech. I wouldn't kill anyone."

"How did you take it when Travis made these statements? Did you believe he was going to kill anyone?"

"No."

After brief testimony by Elwin Ostrander, the service-station owner who had seen Travis block traffic on Main Street while giving Glenn the finger, Hamill called Dave Pallis to the stand. Pallis said he had been a friend of Travis's for eight years. He told of encountering Travis at the Mountain View bar the night of the murder and talking to him for about an hour. Travis drank three beers during that time, Pallis said.

But he testified Travis showed no sign of being drunk—no loss of equilibrium, no loss of hand-eye coordination, no slurring of his speech. Pallis said Travis left the bar before he did.

"What, if anything, occurred just before he left the bar?" Hamill asked.

"He got upset. He got real red. His eyes filled with water."

"Did he say anything?"

"His sister's death wasn't fair."

When Dave Pallis stepped from the stand, Judge Conway adjourned court for the day. By that time it was 4:15 P.M., Thursday, August 6. The trial, including jury selection, had now completed its fourth day.

But the next significant action in the case would not come in the courtroom. It would come at the Best Western Motel in Port Jervis, where the jurors were sequestered overnight.

Juror Patricia Watson tossed in bed at the motel much of the night, unable to sleep. She was worried that her jury service might cause her husband problems at work. Not only did her husband work with Tom Frisch, the witness who had testified he was a close friend of Travis and "loved Kristen Umstadter just like Travis did," but also Frisch's father owned the Wayne County Ready Mix Company, where both the juror's husband and the younger Frisch worked.

Fearing she had made a terrible mistake in agreeing to serve on the jury, Patricia Watson broke into tears and heavy sobs in her motel room. At least one other juror, a roommate, saw her crying. Others would report that she had been striking her head against a wall of the room.

Sheriff's deputies Betty Wood and Gus Geiburg, assigned to

guard the jury, were called to Watson's room. They calmed her, but word of the incident spread. At least part of the jury spent a troubled night.

Judge Conway and the opposing lawyers learned of the bizarre events Friday morning. The judge called the lawyers, the deputies, and selected jurors into his chambers to try to sort out the developments and decide whether the trial could continue. He asked Deputy Geiburg what had happened at the motel.

Geiburg said Watson had come out of her room at about 1:00 A.M. "She was visibly upset, crying, and sobbing," he said. "I went over there and asked her what the problem was, if she was ill or whatever. She was just sobbing and carrying on. I tried to comfort her and calm her down. And she said, 'My husband works there.' I thought she wanted to get in touch with him for something that came up."

The judge asked: "Was there any mention of this murder case or anything like that?"

"No," Geiburg said. "She said, 'I just hope I haven't messed everything up.' Something like that."

"How long did this incident take?" Conway asked.

"Well, she was crying and sobbing," Geiburg said. "I took her for a little walk down the hallway to where my chair was. I said, 'Would you like to sit down for a while?' She said, 'Yes.' And we talked. I said, 'You cannot talk to me about the trial, if that is the problem. You'll have to wait until morning. I'll get in touch with people and get help for you if you need it.' After a while, she agreed that she was feeling better." Watson then returned to her room.

Judge Conway next questioned Deputy Wood. She said Watson was still upset at 6:00 A.M., told her she had been awake since four o'clock, and was concerned over how her husband would feel about her jury service.

Krause asked Wood whether Watson had mentioned any evidence during her outburst. The deputy said she had not.

"Did her roommate see this?" Krause asked.

"Yes, she did," Wood said.

"Did her roommate overhear the conversation she had with you this morning?"

"I would say she did."

The roommate, juror Nancy Martone, was then called in and questioned. She told of Watson bursting into tears and saying that somebody who testified was a friend of her husband's.

The judge asked: "Did you discuss any evidence or testimony with her?"

"I didn't talk to her," Martone said. "I left the room. I told her I didn't want to stay. I didn't want to hear anything." Later, Martone said, another juror told her Watson "was hitting her head against the wall."

In the end, Patricia Watson herself was called to the judge's chambers for questioning. She said she had started wondering during the night what effect the outcome of the trial might have on her husband's friendship with Tom Frisch. She did not mention that her husband worked for Frisch's father, but everyone in the room knew it. While being questioned as a prospective juror, Watson said, she had not considered the situation a problem. But now she was greatly troubled by it.

"Can you get ahold of yourself and listen to the testimony?" Conway asked.

"I don't think I can," Watson replied.

The judge asked the jurors and deputies to leave the room so he and the lawyers could discuss their predicament. Immediately after they left, Lee Krause asked for a mistrial. He argued that all the commotion could distract the jurors and prevent them from properly discharging their duties.

"Denied," Judge Conway said.

"Your Honor, in view of the testimony of Mrs. Watson, I would request that she be excused as a juror and that the first alternate replace her," Krause said.

"No objection from the Commonwealth," Hamill said.

"Granted," the judge ordered.

Watson was driven home. Timothy Jones, the first alternate juror, took her place. For the duration of the trial, there would be only one remaining alternate.

When testimony resumed, Hamill called to the stand probation officer Linus Myers—who had interviewed Glenn Evans shortly before his death and then helped transport Glenn's body from the murder scene to the funeral home. Myers did not mention the trip to his father's mortuary in his testimony, confining himself to the presentencing investigation he had begun conducting in Glenn's case before the murder made it moot.

Hamill asked Myers what Glenn's possible sentence would have been as a result of his conviction in Kristen's death.

"The two major charges were involuntary manslaughter and homicide by vehicle," Myers said. "Both of those counts were punishable by a maximum of five years' imprisonment, a ten-thousand-dollar fine, or both."

Krause asked him on cross-examination: "Would your recommendation have been the maximum sentence?"

"Highly improbable," Myers replied. But he explained later that his recommendation would not have been binding on the judge.

When Myers testified that Glenn expressed remorse over Kristen's death, Krause asked: "These expressions of remorse, that is a common thing that individuals do when they're interviewed—to look for a good report from you—isn't that true?"

"Not all the time, Mr. Krause," Myers said.

Q. I didn't say all the time. I asked if it was a common event.

A. Common event?

Q. More often than not, isn't it?

A. I honestly can't say that. A person's feelings of remorse, I feel, are a very important aspect of a presentence investigation.

Q. That wasn't the question I asked of you, Mr. Myers. I asked if it was more often than not when you are interviewing a defendant who's been convicted that he expresses remorse to you.

A. I would say more often than not.

Q. That's right. That would be more the typical than the atypical, would it not?

A. Sixty-forty.

Q. Have you kept statistics on it?

A. It is not unusual at all, Mr. Krause, to have somebody totally remorseful.

Q. Okay. Mr. Myers, let me ask it this way. Have you found in your experience that people tend to make self-serving statements because they know that this is being used by you to make a recommendation for sentencing?

A. Some do.

"Thank you very much, Mr. Myers," Krause said. "You have been very helpful."

Hamill next called the witness potentially most damaging to Travis's defense—Glenn's girlfriend, Jeanne Marie Coscia. Krause had been trying since even before the start of the trial to persuade the judge to bar Jeanne Marie's testimony. He contended Jeanne Marie's account of her telephone conversation with Glenn on the night of the murder was inadmissible hearsay. But Conway had repeatedly ruled against him.

Now Krause renewed the argument. "I would reiterate my objections," he said. "I have given the court case law on the reasoning." He called Jeanne Marie's prospective testimony "unreliable in itself, hearsay, and inadmissible."

But Judge Conway was unmoved. "Thank you for renewing," he said. "But the same ruling: Objection overruled."

Jeanne Marie appeared fragile in the witness chair—a slender, dark-haired young woman with a delicate, narrow face. Hamill asked her age.

"Eighteen," she said softly—so softly that, moments later, the judge would ask her to speak up. She said she had been a student at the University of Kutztown in Kutztown, Pennsylvania, but was working during the summer as a waitress at the restaurant outside Honesdale called Mustard's Last Stand.

Jeanne Marie testified that in the course of dating Glenn she had visited his apartment at least twenty times. Her last visit, she said, was at about ten-thirty on the night of the murder. She and a friend, Jenny Guardis, stopped at the apartment on the way home from a ski trip. Jeanne Marie said that she and Glenn talked about the trip and that she and Jenny left after about a half-hour.

"Before you left, did you make any arrangements to call or see Glenn again?" Hamill asked.

"Yes, I did," Jeanne Marie said. "He told me to call him when I got home to make sure I got home okay."

"And when you got home did you call Glenn right away?"

"No. I was just getting ready for bed and it was midnight, so I called him then."

"How long did you talk with Glenn that night?"

"Approximately an hour."

Q. Did anything interrupt that conversation at all?

A. Yes. I heard a loud noise. Glenn told me that he thought someone was at the door. As he was walking away—he put the phone down—he told me to hold on a minute. As he started to walk away from the phone, I heard another loud bang. I heard Glenn say: "What the hell are you doing here?"

Q. What was the next thing you heard?

A. Glenn walked back. He picked up the phone and he told me Travis Umstadter was there and he was, like, going to kick his ass.

Q. Did you say anything to Glenn in response to that?

A. I asked him to wake his brother Mark up. He told me when I first called that Mark was in the bed, sleeping.

Q. What, if anything else, was said in the phone conversation?

A. He told me to call him back in about an hour and he'd let me know what happened.

Q. Did you call him back then?

A. No, I did not make the phone call.

Q. Why not?

A. Because I fell asleep on the couch.

Lee Krause took over on cross-examination and asked Jeanne Marie if she had been in love with Glenn. "Yes," she replied. Krause then established that there had been no witnesses to Jeanne Marie's end of the phone conversation. Jeanne Marie testified that her mother, brother, and two sisters were in the house at the time but that all were asleep.

Krause questioned her sharply about her testimony that she had simply fallen asleep and failed to call Glenn back. "Now, you knew, did you not, that Kristen Umstadter was killed in this automobile accident?" he asked.

"Yes," Jeanne Marie said.

"And you knew who Travis was, didn't you?"

"Yes."

"And you heard the statement from your boyfriend that it looked like Travis was there to kick my ass, right?"

"Yes."

"And you're in love with this fellow, right?"

"Yes."

"You mean to tell me you fell asleep? You didn't wake your mother up, call the state police, run out there yourself? You just fell asleep on the couch? Is that what happened?"

"I knew Mark was there and I didn't think there'd be a problem," Jeanne Marie said.

"Okay. But you didn't call anybody or tell anybody? You fell asleep after this conversation and you never called him back the rest of the evening?"

"No, I did not."

Krause asked Jeanne Marie if she talked to Allan Rutledge about Glenn's murder shortly after it was committed. She said she could not remember. If Krause hoped to draw from her an admission that she had actually accused Rutledge of the murder, as Rutledge claimed, he was destined for disappointment. No matter how closely he questioned her, Jeanne Marie insisted that she could not recall talking to Rutledge after Glenn's death.

"I have no other questions of the witness," Krause said.

Ray Hamill rose and stepped before the bench. "Your

Honor, that concludes the list of witnesses the Commonwealth would call," he said. "The Commonwealth rests."

Judge Conway called the lawyers into his chambers. Krause immediately moved for dismissal of the most serious charge against Travis, first-degree murder.

"None of the evidence has established murder in the first degree sufficient to go to the jury," Krause argued. "There is no physical evidence whatsoever in the apartment, on the gun, or as a result of any of the tests the state police have taken that Travis Umstadter was present in the apartment. The only testimony that places Travis Umstadter at the scene of the crime is the testimony of Jeanne Marie Coscia, whose testimony I originally objected to on what I believe are proper grounds."

Krause described Jeanne Marie's testimony as "incredible." And if it were disregarded, he said, the first-degree-murder charge could not stand.

Hamill, not unexpectedly, argued to the contrary. "Your Honor, the gun was found in the defendant's vehicle," he said. "It was the gun that fired the four fatal shots in the head. It was in his possession that night, seen by Doug Smith in the car just hours before the homicide. I believe that, if we had nothing else, that would be sufficient evidence to go to the jury. We do have, however, preannounced intention to kill. We also have Jeanne Marie Coscia's statement. I believe the Commonwealth has made out a prima facie case for the jury."

The judge turned to Krause. "Motion denied," he ruled.

TWELVE

"Call Laraine Umstadter," Lee Krause said when the trial resumed.

Krause was leading from strength, calling his most imposing witness to the stand at the outset of the defense case. Krause considered Laraine the dominant figure in the Umstadter household—the one who made the wheels turn. An outer air of fragility notwithstanding, Laraine was an exceedingly tough woman. There was steel in her blue eyes. There was sadness as well, of course. How could there not be for a mother whose daughter had been killed in one tragedy and whose son faced possible life imprisonment in another? But the countenance Laraine showed the world through all this adversity had seemed characterized less by sadness than by an icy fury. Krause planned to try to demonstrate that Travis had been influenced by his mother's attitude and by her constant pressure to resolve the supposed unanswered questions surrounding Kristen's death.

Laraine sat uneasily in the witness chair, her legs crossed. The muscles in her face were drawn taut. Her blond bangs fell low over her forehead.

Krause began with a series of housekeeping questions—where Laraine lived, the size of her family. "Your daughter's name?" he asked.

"Kristen," Laraine said.

"Is Kristen living now?"

"No, she is not."

"Now, do you know how your daughter died?"

"Yes, I do. In a violent car crash."

"Who was driving the car?"

"Glenn Evans."

"What happened to your family after that accident?"

"We were really devastated. She was probably the center of the family."

Asked to describe the relationship between Travis and Kristen, Laraine answered: "I think they had an unusually close relationship for a brother and sister. They were very close in age and had a lot of the same interests and friends, a lot of the same activities, spent a lot of time together.

> Q. Mrs. Umstadter, after your daughter's death, did you have any unanswered questions about her death?
> A. Many.
> Q. Did you express that to anyone in your family?
> A. We all talked about it constantly.
> Q. Where did these discussions take place?
> A. Mostly at the kitchen table.

Krause tried to enter in evidence the portrait of Kristen that had hung on a wall, in full view of the Umstadters, during these discussions. He said the portrait was relevant because it affected Travis's state of mind during the period leading to the shooting. Hamill objected to its introduction. "I've got to believe that represents nothing more than an attempt to make Kristen Umstadter the victim in this whole case," he said. Judge Conway upheld the objection.

When Krause asked Laraine to describe the unanswered questions about Kristen's death, she specified only one of the many she harbored. "We feel that Kristen was coaxed into the car," Laraine testified. "And I wanted to know if that was true —if she had put herself in the car of her own wishes or if somebody had coaxed her to go."

"And you had these conversations with Travis?" Krause asked.

"Yes."

Q. Now, did you ever tell Travis that you wanted answers to these questions?

A. Yes, I did. On many, many occasions.

Q. Was this a topic of conversation in your home every night since your daughter's death?

A. More nights than not.

Q. Did you ask Travis questions when he would return home at the end of the working day?

A. Yes. I'd ask him if anyone had said anything to him or if he had seen Glenn Evans.

Q. Did you engender an animosity toward Glenn Evans yourself?

A. Yes.

Q. Did you make that known to Travis?

A. Yes, I did.

Laraine testified that Travis's drinking increased "a great deal" after Kristen's death. Asked to describe how Travis looked and acted when drunk, Laraine said: "He speaks with a drawn lip. He kind of stretches his lip and it's also a little hard to understand but I can always tell when he's been drinking by the way he talks. And he cries. And I would say he probably is a little irrational, angry. He says things that don't really make too much sense."

On the day leading to the shooting, Laraine testified, she returned home from work at about 5:00 P.M. Since Travis's car was not at the house, she assumed he had come home from work and then gone somewhere. The next time she saw him, she said, was when he burst into the house at two-thirty in the morning—sobbing and muttering something about Glenn Evans.

"He was very upset and he was drunk and crying," Laraine said. "He reeked, just reeked, of alcohol. And he was crying and his eyes were red—could be from the crying, you know—but he was visibly drunk."

Laraine said she repeatedly asked Travis for an explanation of what had happened but could get only disconnected refer-ences to Glenn and then to Travis's gun. She told of telephoning Krause, of his arrival at the house, and the summoning of the state police.

Shifting back to the events preceding the shooting, Krause asked Laraine: "Mrs. Umstadter, did your family's grief heighten at any time during the trial of Glenn Evans?"

"Yes, it did," Laraine said. "Prior to the trial we heard many stories that he was going to get off because it wasn't his fault and that it was Kristen's own fault that she was dead. We were very upset about the comments that were coming back."

Q. He wasn't convicted of all charges? And you were upset as a result of that?

A. Yes, we were.

Q. Was Travis upset?

A. Yes.

Q. Did you make your feelings known to him also?

A. I'm sure we all knew each other's feelings in the house about the whole thing.

Q. Did that trial answer the questions that you told the jury that you asked of yourself and of Travis about your daughter's death?

A. No, it did not.

"Thank you," Krause said. "I have no further questions."

Ray Hamill, on cross-examination, asked Laraine only a few questions—chiefly concerning her reaction to the circumstances of Kristen's death. At Glenn's trial, hadn't she heard Kristen's friends testify about how they all came to be in Glenn's car? And hadn't she heard Glenn himself tell what had led Kristen to enter the car?

"I don't believe he told all of it," Laraine said adamantly.

The issue remained unresolved as Laraine was excused and succeeded in the witness chair by her husband. When Krause asked him how many children he had, Dave Umstadter replied: "Three."

"Is one deceased?"

"I beg your pardon, two," Dave said. "I'm a nervous wreck."

Dave testified he shared his wife's questions about Kristen's death. "I found it hard to believe, which I still find it hard to believe, that Kristen was in that car at all," he said. "And I indicated to Travis on many occasions that I felt there were a lot of things that were untold in the story. I feel she was coaxed in the car."

"Now, did you yourself express any personal animosity toward Glenn Evans?" Krause asked.

"Yes, indeed, I did."

"Did Travis have questions also?"

"Yes, he did. Kristen would not get in the car with Travis, her brother, when he had been drinking, and she absolutely refused and cried over it."

Hamill was on his feet, objecting that Dave's answer had not been responsive to the question. "Sustained," the judge ruled. "The jury is told to disregard the witness's answer to the question."

Krause gently admonished Dave. "Mr. Umstadter, you'll have to listen to my question," he said. "I know you're nervous. You indicated that it's difficult for you. But try to answer the questions as I pose them to you."

Moving to the night of the shooting, Krause asked Dave to describe Travis's appearance when he came home. Dave said Travis was crying, smelled of alcohol, and seemed drunk.

"Could you make any sense out of statements he was making?"

"Not a whole lot."

On cross-examination, Hamill took Dave back over the issue of the unanswered questions in Kristen's death. "You attended the trial?" Hamill asked.

"Yes, I did."

"You heard the sworn testimony of the friends?"

"Yes, I did."

"And they explained how it was that your daughter came to be in that car, correct?"

"I heard what they said."

"And they were sworn and under oath?"

"Yes, they were."

"And they were your daughter's friends, were they not?"

"Acquaintances."

"I have no further questions, Your Honor," Hamill said.

Travis's friend Cord Meyer then testified about encountering him in the Mountain View on the night of the shooting. "I bought him probably between six and eight shots of apple schnapps and we were drinking draft beers with them," Meyer said.

Allan Rutledge followed him to the stand. Under Krause's questioning, Rutledge testified that he had been a close friend of both Travis and Kristen ever since the Umstadter family moved to the Honesdale area. He told of his romance with Kristen.

"What happened to that relationship, if anything?" Krause asked.

"I left for the Navy July twenty-third, 1986, and that is when the accident happened," Rutledge said.

"You never saw her again, is that right?"

"No."

Rutledge said he, Travis, and their friends all drank more after Kristen's death than they had in the past. "It was a way to forget," he testified.

"Did you ever say in the presence of Travis that Glenn didn't get enough and he ought to be killed?" Krause asked.

"Yes," Rutledge replied.

"More than one occasion?"

"More than once."

"Did you ever plan to kill him?"

"No. It was just something that we talked about. There was never any plan of going after him or anything like that. It was just talk."

"Why were you upset with Glenn Evans?"

"Because he took something away from all of us."

Krause then took Rutledge through an account of the telephone call he said he received from Jeanne Marie Coscia shortly after Glenn's murder. Rutledge said Jeanne Marie seemed to be looking for a shoulder to cry on and trying to figure out what had happened. "She went on to talk about who could do such a thing," he said. "That went on until I hung up on her."

Rutledge said a friend of Jeanne Marie's, Lisa Coweger, had also come on the phone during the conversation. "They took turns on the phone and they thought I had done it and both of them accused me of it over the phone," he said. "When Jeanne Marie asked who could do such a thing, I asked: 'Who wouldn't?' Then both of them accused me of doing it."

"In that phone conversation, did Jeanne Marie mention Travis Umstadter's name?" Krause asked.

"Not once," Rutledge replied.

"Did she mention that she had a phone conversation with Glenn Evans and that Travis was at the apartment the night he was killed?"

"No. That didn't come up until three or four months later, when I talked to her again."

Krause next called back to the stand county coroner Young W. Lee, hoping to bolster the contention that Travis was too drunk at the time of the shooting to form the criminal intent necessary for a first-degree-murder conviction. Based on the blood test taken the morning of the murder, Lee estimated that Travis's blood-alcohol content at about the time of the shooting was in the vicinity of .18—almost double the legal intoxication level.

Asked to describe the symptoms a drinker would exhibit if his alcohol content were in that range, Lee testified: "Reaction time is greatly prolonged. Then loss of inhibitions and slight disturbance of equilibrium. A little bit wobbly or whatever. And then slightly disturbed coordination."

Since Lee conceded his .18 figure was merely an estimate, Krause asked what the symptoms would be if the drinker's alcohol content were .20 or higher. "Disturbance of equilibrium and coordination, retardation of the thought process, and clouding of consciousness," the coroner replied.

Throughout the trial, Lee Krause had been playing a cagy little game—keeping his own counsel over whether Travis would take the stand. At various points he had indicated Travis would indeed testify. But then he had appeared to hedge—noting there was no obligation on a defendant even to present a defense, much less take the stand.

Now Krause put an end to the suspense. "Your Honor, at this time I call the defendant, Travis Umstadter," he said.

Travis seemed plainly nervous as he sank into the witness chair. There was no trace of the expression he often showed the world—what Krause calls Travis's macho face. Even for a man on trial on a first-degree-murder charge, Travis appeared uncommonly vulnerable.

After trying to settle him down with a few routine questions, Krause asked Travis to describe his relationship with Kristen. "We were more than brother and sister," Travis said. "We were best of friends, actually. It was extremely close."

As for Glenn Evans, Travis told of going to school with him and getting along with him until Kristen's death. "We never had a bad word between us," he said. "I mean, we weren't great friends, but we got along."

"Okay," Krause said. "Now, after Kristen's death, would you describe what effect, if any, that had on you?"

"I had anxiety and hurt," Travis replied. "I was unable to believe it. Every day, I waited for her to come home. I waited for her to call, something. I didn't understand why she was gone. I had so many questions."

Q. What kind of questions did you have?

A. I couldn't understand that she was out drinking and riding around. She talked to me about personal things and more things than she talked to anyone in my family. And I knew her.

Q. All right, Travis. What questions now remained unanswered in your mind after her death?

A. Why she was in the car. Why her car was unlocked with the keys in it. Her purse in the car, which is something she never did—never. When her car was at home, it wasn't unlocked. And she had just been paid that Friday afternoon, and the next morning, when we got the car, she didn't have a cent in her wallet. There was nothing there. And there is no way she could spend a week's pay in a few hours.

Q. Did your family have questions, too?

A. Yes, they did.

Q. How often did you discuss these unanswered questions with your family after Kristen's death?

A. Every day, sometimes twice a day. It was always there. I had pressure from my parents because I was out and around more places than most people in my family.

Travis was struggling to hold back tears. "Okay, Travis, take it easy," Krause urged.

"My mother, every day, was asking me what did I hear," Travis testified. He said Laraine was sometimes angry and often cried during these conversations.

Krause asked whether the testimony at Glenn's trial had resolved any of the questions about Kristen's death. "No, it did not," Travis said. "I didn't feel the truth came out in the trial. Under oath or not under oath, in my opinion they all lied."

After taking Travis through the history of his illegal underage drinking, Krause asked him if he continued to drink after Glenn's trial. "Yes, I did," Travis replied.

"Why was that?" Krause asked.

"Because if I got drunk enough then all I wanted to do was sleep. All I wanted to do was just go home and not think about things, not have to worry about it."

Q. Did you have discussions with friends of yours? You have heard their testimony here that you wanted to get Glenn Evans or kill him?

A. Yes, I did say that.

Q. Did you ever form a plan to kill him?

A. No, I didn't. I never wanted to kill anyone. Never. I'm not a killer.

Q. Okay. Take it easy. Travis, did any of your friends say the same thing to you?

A. Most all my friends and Kristen's friends thought that he should pay in one way or another. And some of them, yes, said they'd like to kill him.

Q. Did you believe they had a plan or anyone was going to kill him?

A. I never believed anyone was literally going to go out and kill this man.

Krause then drew from Travis a chronology of the hours preceding the shooting—his return from work, his drive to his family's then-incomplete house near Lookout, his first stop at the Mountain View bar, his long ride with Dougie Smith, his problem with the gun sliding free when he jammed on the brakes, his return to the Mountain View. Travis described all the drinking he had done during the night. When Krause questioned him about his conversation with Dave Pallis during the second stop at the Mountain View, Travis said he was drunk at the time and could not remember everything that was said.

"Do you remember crying at the bar? What brought that on?"

"Somehow, my sister got on my mind. I talked a little bit about her to Dave and he tried to change the subject, tried to cheer me up some. When he couldn't, I just left my beer on the bar and I left."

"You were crying. You left. Where'd you go?"

"I headed home, south on One-Ninety-One."

"How did you feel?"

"I felt upset and I had trouble driving. I almost got stuck in the snow between Lookout and Honesdale. And I just—all I wanted to do was get home and go to bed. I had to get up early to go to work."

Travis told of his gun sliding off the seat and coming partly out of its holster while he was maneuvering the car free of the snow. Krause asked why he carried a gun in the car. "Well, I'm a woodsman, sportsman, and I do a lot of trapping," Travis said. "And it's also hard to carry a rifle when you are trying to carry furs on one shoulder and traps over the other. So a handgun was a lot more convenient. I could carry it on my side and still be able to do my work."

"Was it always loaded when it was in your car?"

"Yes."

Q. All right, it fell off the seat coming home. What did you do with it?

A. I picked the pistol up—it's without the holster—and stuck it in my waistband.

Q. Had you done that before?

A. Yes, I had because it was a very common occurrence for it to slide out from under the seat. And it gets annoying. So I put it there and I knew it wasn't going anywhere.

Q. What were you wearing at the time?

A. I had a flannel shirt and an insulated flannel shirt over that.

Q. What happened next, Travis?

A. I kept heading home after I got my car back between the ditches, as they say. Somewhere along the course of North Main Street, I started thinking that tomorrow I'm going to have to answer these questions again—that I have been out all night and I still have no answers for my parents. So I turned around. Next thing I knew I remember I was knocking on an apartment door—the apartment building where Glenn Evans lived with his brother.

Q. Did you know what apartment Glenn lived in?

A. No, sir.

Q. All right. So the next thing you knew you were knocking on his door?

A. I didn't know if it was his door. It was the only apartment in the whole building with the lights on. If it wasn't his home, I was going to ask whoever was living there where his apartment was. I had to find out some answers. I

had to get something to settle the questions within me and
my family, so that we could all go on—go on with our lives
and just try to understand it.

Travis testified Glenn answered his knock at the door, let
him in, and offered him a seat at the table in the living-dining
area. Both of them were nervous—"a natural reaction," Travis
said. He asked Glenn to tell him "what really happened" the
night of Kristen's death. They talked for about an hour. Both
were smoking much of the time. Occasionally, Travis said,
Glenn twirled in his fingers a pair of scissors that had been
lying on the table.

Although the conversation was civil at first, Travis testified,
it later turned nasty. The words were not particularly heated,
he said, but sarcastic and biting.

Now Lee Krause set up a graphic demonstration of the sort
usually reserved for courtroom scenes on movie and television
screens. The demonstration was to serve as a vehicle for Travis
to tell publicly for the first time what all of Wayne County had
been waiting months to hear—his version of just how four bullets had come to be fired into the head of Glenn Evans.

The table and chairs from Glenn's apartment were carried
into the courtroom. Krause asked Travis to sit at the place he
had occupied at the table on the night of the shooting. The
items found on the table by the police were produced—an ash-
tray, the scissors, a beer bottle, a pack of cigarettes, and a
lighter. Travis placed each item where it had been on the table,
to his recollection, during his conversation with Glenn. Krause,
after having the murder weapon checked to be sure it was un-
loaded, handed it to Travis and asked him to put it in his
waistband.

"Where was Glenn Evans seated?" Krause asked.

"At the table in the chair to my right," Travis said, indicating a chair at a right angle to his.

"Where would the door to the apartment be?"

"Directly behind me."

"Do you recall all the conversation while you were there?"

"No, I do not."

"Do you recall the end of the conversation?"

"The last few words. I again asked Glenn about my sister, about the true facts. He got very smug, very cocky. And he said: 'I don't know why you bother me with this. If that dumb bitch sister of yours hadn't grabbed the steering wheel, she would be living today.' "

It seemed an explosive piece of testimony. But the jurors' faces betrayed no trace of animation.

"What else did Glenn say?" Krause asked.

"He said he was sick and tired of looks that he was getting from the townspeople, the remarks, the rumors he'd heard as to people wanting to come after him. He just said that he was going to stop it—and he was going to stop it with me."

"Did he do anything?"

Travis's face was contorted in anguish. "Take it easy, Travis," Krause urged.

"I hate this," Travis muttered. "You know that."

"I know."

Belatedly answering the question originally asked, Travis said: "He picked up the scissors."

"Objection," Ray Hamill said.

Krause, appearing surprised, said: "I asked if he did any-thing."

"And then you went to pick up the scissors," Hamill said.

"Yes, I did."

"Sustained," the judge told Krause. "You're not part of this. Just ask the question, Mr. Krause."

The defense lawyer had hoped to enact Glenn Evans's role during the remainder of the demonstration. But the judge's ruling made that impossible.

"What did Glenn do?" Krause asked.

"He picked the scissors up and, like, rose across the table and swung them at my eyes and my face in general," Travis said, swinging his right arm to show what Glenn had suppos-edly done.

Q. He stood up?

A. He was half leaning across the table.

Q. Were these the scissors?

A. Yes.

Q. Where were they directed? ___

A. Toward my face, my eyes.

Q. How close were they to your eyes?

A. Too close.

Q. What did you do when Glenn Evans thrust these scissors at your eyes?

A. When he first swiped at them, I protected myself the only way I knew how. I pulled my revolver and I shot him.

Q. Do you know how many times you shot him, sitting here today?

A. No. Only from the testimony that he was shot four times. I didn't know.

Krause walked up to the table. "You were about this close—as close as you and I are—when this occurred?"

"Yes."

"And you took the gun. Show the jury how you took the gun."

"It was all so fast," Travis said. "I pulled it. I don't want to do this."

"Okay. All right. Travis—"

"I can't do this," Travis insisted.

"Travis, you do recall a shot or shooting? You don't know how many?"

"No, I don't."

"Take the gun out of your pants," Krause instructed. "Back up and take the stand."

When Travis handed over the gun and returned to the witness stand, Krause asked: "What happened after you shot him?"

"I saw him start to fall and I left," Travis said. "I didn't know if he was dead or alive. I didn't even know if I hit him or if he was ducking."

Q. Where did you go? What did you do?

A. I went home and woke up my parents. I was upset. They both tried to calm me down. My brother came out of the bedroom, trying to calm me down. Mom kept asking me: "What's wrong? What's wrong?" And she was shaking me by my shoulders. I kept getting dizzy. I couldn't tell her anything. I couldn't tell her anything.

Only later, Glenn said, did he settle down enough to tell his mother he had gone to Glenn's. Krause took him through the arrival of the state police and the first day of the investigation.

Q. Travis, immediately after the shooting, did you have any independent recollection of what happened—the next day even?

A. By the next day, I knew that I had shot him. How, I didn't know. Why, I didn't know. I racked my brains because I didn't understand. I didn't know why.

Q. Was there a time you believed you didn't shoot him?

A. At times I did believe it was not me. I didn't believe I was capable. I couldn't piece together doing it or why I did it. The doubt did come to me as to whether I did shoot him or not.

Q. When did it come so that you could recollect the events you just described to this jury?

A. Not until maybe two, two and a half weeks later when you showed me photographs of the apartment and of the body, Glenn's. It started coming together. I started seeing different things that had been somehow blocked out of my memory. I saw a picture of the scissors and it all came back so fast it was like a flash. It was there. I was speechless a few seconds. I shook. I couldn't believe that it was all really happening.

Q. Travis, have you sought psychiatric help after this incident?

A. Yes.

Q. And have you been seeing someone in Scranton?

A. Yes, I have—Dr. John Lesniak.
Q. Why? Why do you see him?

"Objection," Ray Hamill said.
"Sustained," Judge Conway ruled.
"How often have you seen him?" Krause asked.
"Objection, Your Honor."
"Sustained."

It would not be the last time Krause would be frustrated in an attempt to establish a psychiatric defense. Throughout the remainder of the trial, he would find Judge Conway sharply restricting the scope of questions dealing with psychiatric issues.

Krause shifted gears. "Travis, did you go up there that night with the intent to kill Glenn Evans?" he asked.

"No, sir, I did not," Travis replied. "I never wanted to kill anyone in my life."

Q. Even though you said you wanted him dead?
A. Even though I have said that. I never wanted to kill anyone. I know what it is like to lose a member of a family.
Q. Why did you shoot him?
A. I was trying to get away from him. I was trying to protect my life.
Q. Where was the gun when you got home?
A. Apparently in the car. I didn't know.
Q. You didn't throw it away?
A. No.

Actually, if Travis *had* thrown the gun away and it had not been discovered, he might never have come to trial. Ray Hamill and Herman Todd concede the absence of the gun could have short-circuited the prosecution. Without the gun, they would have had no physical evidence whatever connecting Travis with the crime. Hamill just rolls his eyes in mere contemplation of what might have confronted him. Todd is more direct. "It would have been tough sledding for sure," he says.

But Travis had not disposed of the gun. And now Lee Krause was asking more questions about it. "Did you ever threaten Glenn Evans with the gun at all?"

Travis said Glenn did not even know he had the gun, since it was covered by his outer shirt.

"Did you ever show it to him before he struck at you with these scissors?"

"No, I did not."

"How do you feel about his death now?" Krause asked.

Travis, his eyes brimming with tears, replied: "I see him die every day. And I feel myself dying more every day. I know this may not mean much, but I sympathize with his family. I'm— I'm sorry. I never wanted to kill anybody."

Krause knew when to quit. "Thank you very much, Travis," he said. "Your witness."

Ray Hamill began his cross-examination with a direct assault on the defense contention that Travis was too drunk the night of the shooting to form the criminal intent needed for a first-degree-murder conviction. Questioning him intensely about his drinking habits, the DA sought to demonstrate that Travis could consume large quantities of alcohol without losing the ability to function.

"When did you start drinking alcoholic beverages?" Hamill asked.

"I was about fourteen," Travis replied. At that age, he said, two beers were enough to get him drunk. But, year by year, his capacity increased.

> Q. Isn't it true, Mr. Umstadter, that by the time of your sister's death you were able to drink a case of beer starting in the afternoon and going into the early-morning hours?
>
> A. Yes, that is true.
>
> Q. And on those occasions you would be driving a car around often at night, wouldn't you?
>
> A. Sometimes.
>
> Q. And you found that if you drank more and more beer that you were able to navigate that car, didn't you?

A. Actually, no. I wrecked every car I ever owned.

Q. But you kept on drinking the beer? And driving?

A. Yes.

Q. Would you have us believe that your ability to handle alcohol didn't get better over the course of time?

A. To be honest with you, I believe I have a drinking problem.

Q. You would drink a case of beer and you wouldn't even pass out, would you?

A. Nope.

Q. You would mix beer and other kinds of alcohol and not pass out, wouldn't you?

A. No. Usually, if I drank enough of both, it would pretty much put me under.

Under Hamill's questioning, Travis then reviewed the drinking he had done the night of the shooting—beginning with at least six shots of apple schnapps and two or three beers during his first visit to the Mountain View. He agreed with Dougie Smith's testimony that the two of them had finished three six-packs of beer during their ride, but his recollection was that he had drunk considerably more of the beer than Dougie had. Then, Travis said, he had another beer on his second stop at the Mountain View.

Hamill next traced Travis's movements after leaving the Mountain View the second time—his drive toward home, his U-turn on Main Street, and the turn onto Route 6 toward Glenn's apartment.

"Where were you going?" Hamill asked.

"I didn't know," Travis said. But then he corrected that. He said he remembered telling himself that he had to get answers to the questions about Kristen's death. "So I guess I did know," he said.

"So you did know where you were going when you turned the car around on Main Street?" Hamill asked.

"Yes, sir."

"So you did know from that point forward that you were

going to Glenn Evans's apartment to get some answers, didn't you?"

"Yes, sir, I did."

"And you knew you had the gun in your waistband?"

"Yes, sir, I did."

"You said you were really upset about your sister's death?"

"Yes, sir."

Wasn't it true, Hamill asked, that Travis had stopped drinking temporarily after Kristen's death? Correct, Travis said. "I felt I owed it to myself."

Well, Hamill pressed, wasn't his sister always getting on his back about his drinking? True, Travis conceded. And hadn't his abstention lasted only a week?

"Approximately a week, yes," Travis said.

"And, when you started up again, didn't you tell people the reason that you started drinking again was because Chrissy would want you to get on with your life?" Hamill asked.

"No, sir, that is not true."

"You didn't tell people that Chrissy wouldn't want you—"

Travis interrupted him. "Excuse me, sir, but her name was Kristen," he said.

"Sorry," Hamill told him.

"I'm sorry, but it hurts."

"Kristen," Hamill said.

"Thanks."

"If I rephrased it to Kristen, would your answer still be the same?"

"Yes. I told people that Kristen was a very free-spirited person and that she would not have wanted anyone to be crying over her death."

Now Hamill began his own reenactment of the shooting. The table and chairs from Glenn's apartment were still in the courtroom. Hamill walked to the spot at the table where Travis said Glenn had been seated.

"You told us Glenn Evans was sitting here at this chair," he said.

"Yes, sir."

"Tell me if I do anything wrong. You told us that he picked up the scissors and swung at you, right?"

"Yes, I did."

Hamill picked up the scissors in his right hand and made a stabbing motion at face height. "Just like that, right at you?" he asked.

"Yes, sir," Travis said.

"I didn't do anything wrong in that illustration, did I?"

"Glenn was half standing up, leaning over the table."

"I'm going to go back and do it again," Hamill said. "You stop me and you tell me that I'm in the proper position to re-create the scene."

"Objection," Lee Krause said. "If I can't re-create the scene and become an actor, how can the other counsel?"

Judge Conway ruled such a demonstration was permissible on cross-examination. Hamill resumed his reenactment.

"Picks up the scissors, right?" Hamill asked Travis. "Tell me when to stop."

"I can't tell you when to stop," Travis said. "It all happened in one instant."

"He swung at you?" Hamill asked, slicing the air with his right arm.

"Yes, sir," Travis replied.

"You ducked back?"

"Yes, sir, I did."

"You fall out of the chair?"

"I stumbled over it as I stood up," Travis said. "Me and Glenn were both moving at the same time. He came at me. I backed away."

"Did you knock the chair over?"

"No, sir."

"So you knocked the chair backwards, but it didn't fall over?"

"True."

Hamill asked for further details on the conversation preceding the violence. Travis said Glenn talked about the accident but told him nothing new. Well, hadn't Glenn said that Kristen had entered his car voluntarily? No, Travis testified. "I never asked him that."

Seemingly incredulous, Hamill asked him: "Wasn't that one of the most important questions you had?" Travis replied that it "ranked up there" but that he hadn't gotten around to asking it before Glenn came at him with the scissors.

Q. After he lunged at you with the scissors, you stood up. You backed up. Right?

A. Yes, sir.

Q. Was it then that you pulled the gun out?

A. I don't know.

Q. Do you remember you shot him with your gun?

A. I guess, yes.

Q. I don't want you to guess. Do you remember shooting him with your gun?

A. My gun was the gun that was on me at the time. Yes, sir, I remember.

Q. Do you remember shooting him with your gun? Do you remember aiming that gun?

A. No, sir, I didn't aim the gun. The gun wasn't even sighted in.

Asked if Glenn was smoking at the time, Travis said he didn't know. He had no explanation for the blood-smeared cigarette discovered beneath Glenn's body. And, although the evidence clearly showed four bullet holes in Glenn's body, Travis said he had no recollection of pulling the revolver's trigger or hammer four times. Hamill asked if he remembered what he did just before running from Glenn's apartment.

"I remember the first shot and I remember him falling and I remember leaving," Travis said.

"Let's talk about the first shot. Did you see where the first shot entered his body?"

"I didn't know if I hit him or not. He fell. I didn't know if he was ducking or he was going—"

Q. He took a swipe at your eyes. You stood up. You shot. He fell to the floor. That's where your memory ends?

A. No. Obviously, I fired the gun more than once. I remember him on the floor and I remember leaving. That does not mean he fell to the floor on the first shot.

Q. Do you remember what happened to Glenn Evans's body after your first shot?

A. No.

Q. So, for all you know, Glenn Evans's head went back and came down on the table in his arms?

A. I don't know.

Q. For all you know, you stood over the body and took another shot at the back of Glenn Evans's head. And his body fell over, bringing blood across the table, for all you know?

A. No. I don't believe I would act that way, sir. I'm sorry.

Q. For all you know and recollect, you took one last shot as he lay on the floor?

A. No, sir. All I know is I protected my life. How many times I shot him, I don't know. But I would never stand over a person and shoot into him. Never.

Q. He still have the scissors in his hand when you shot him the first time?

A. I believe he did.

Q. He had just taken a swipe at you, hadn't he?

A. Yes, sir.

"No further questions," Hamill said, leaving it for the jury to decide how the scissors wound up on the table if they were in Glenn's hand when he was shot. They could have fallen there, of course. But they also could have fallen elsewhere or could have remained in Glenn's hand—assuming, in the first place, that Travis's story was true.

The question was left hanging as Lee Krause walked toward his client. "Travis, I think you've had enough," Krause said. "No redirect."

Travis, his eyes red and his body trembling slightly, walked unsteadily back to the defense table. Minutes later, the trial adjourned for the day. Judge Conway called Hamill and Krause into his chambers.

There, Krause sought permission from the judge to call two psychiatrists to the stand the next day as his final substantive witnesses. Both had examined Travis and concluded he was suffering from a mental disorder at the time of the shooting. Krause described the disorder as a combination of anxiety, depression, and the effects of heavy drinking. "This would greatly affect his ability to carry out a plan or design," the defense attorney said.

Hamill objected to the proposed testimony. He argued that in order for a defendant to make a claim of diminished mental capacity, he must first concede his culpability. "The defendant in this case has just maintained by his very testimony that he acted in self-defense," Hamill said. "That is not a concession of general criminal culpability. The Commonwealth asks the court to refuse to permit the psychiatrists to testify."

Judge Conway ruled that they could not testify about the supposed mental disorder. Krause then asked that one or both of the psychiatrists be permitted to testify strictly on whether Travis's drinking the night of the shooting could have affected his ability to form the criminal intent needed for a first-degree-murder conviction. Hamill offered no objection to that, and the judge said he would permit it.

It was Saturday, August 8. The judge had ordered the trial to continue into the weekend.

Lee Krause had decided to settle for putting one psychiatrist, Dr. John Lesniak, on the stand. Lesniak testified that he had taken special training in treating alcoholics and had directed alcohol-detoxification programs at several hospitals. He was accepted as an expert witness.

Lesniak said he was familiar with the results of the blood-alcohol test made on Travis and the calculations drawn up by county coroner Lee. Krause then asked what sort of behavior could be expected from someone with such test readings.

"The traits that are demonstrated are, first of all, a breakdown of a person's general defenses so that he might demonstrate abnormalities of personality," Lesniak testified. "In other words, you would see a personality that may not be seen if the person is not drinking. In conjunction with this, he may show evidence of aggressiveness, sometimes poor impulse control, and on a physical level you may also see evidence of loss of equilibrium, staggering, and slurred speech."

Q. Now, Doctor, based upon your medical knowledge and the information which you have from your consultations with the defendant, Travis Umstadter, the evidence which has been presented concerning the quantity of alcohol that Travis Umstadter ingested during the course of this evening, do you have an opinion with reasonable medical certainty as to whether Travis Umstadter had the ability to form the specific intent to premeditate the murder of Glenn Evans?

A. Yes, I do. . . . My opinion would be that Travis Umstadter did not have the ability to form that intent.

Q. And this is as a result of the ingestion of alcohol?

A. Yes.

Q. Doctor, would you describe what effect alcohol has on the mind in forming premeditation or thoughts concerning specific intent?

A. Well, with regard to excessive alcohol within the brain, it certainly causes many gaps in making cognitive decisions. The intellect is impaired. People who drink excessively do not think properly and on many occasions they make mistakes in judgment and their insights are impaired so they cannot function on a regular or predictable basis.

Q. Can they still drive a car?

A. They can drive a car but not safely. Up to a certain point.

Q. Can they, given this amount of alcohol, still converse?

"Objection, Your Honor," Hamill said. "This is off the point of specific intent."

"Sustained."

"No further questions," Krause said. Hamill declined to cross-examine.

Krause then called three character witnesses—high school principal Dan O'Neill and two friends of the Umstadter family. All testified that Travis had an excellent reputation in the community for truthfulness.

"The defense rests," Krause said.

But the testimony was not quite over yet. Ray Hamill told the judge he would present two rebuttal witnesses.

The first was Walter Hrynkiw, a state police pharmacologist called in an attempt to minimize the effect of the defense's psychiatric testimony. Based on calculations he had made, Hrynkiw said Travis's drinking on the night of the shooting would not have impaired his functioning so severely as the defense contended. Travis should have retained "good cognition" and there should have been no memory loss, he contended.

Hamill called as his final witness Glenn Evans's twenty-three-year-old brother Frank. Throughout the trial's reenactments of the confrontation between Glenn and Travis, Glenn had consistently been shown swinging the scissors with his right hand. Hamill had asked Travis to correct anything that seemed inaccurate in these reenactments, but Travis had said nothing about the position of the scissors.

Now, Hamill asked Frank Evans: "Was Glenn right-handed or left-handed?"

"Left-handed," Evans replied.

"No further questions," Hamill said.

Without question, that testimony hurt the defense. But Krause tried to cut the loss on cross-examination.

"Mr. Evans, have you seen your brother use both hands?" he asked.

"Yes."

"In other words, he was not disabled with regard to his right hand. Is that right?"

"No."

"And did you see him pick things up with his right hand?"

"Yes, he used his right hand at times."

"Thank you very much."

That was it. The testimony in the case was over.

Judge Conway adjourned court for the remainder of the weekend. The jurors would be taken back to the Port Jervis motel until it was time for them to appear in court the following Monday morning.

It was a tense weekend for all the trial's participants, but especially for the Umstadters. Travis spent what might be his last hours alone with his bride for a long time. If the jury's decision went against him, he could be confronted with instant imprisonment.

Before Judge Conway took the bench Monday morning, he met still again in his chambers with Krause and Hamill. Krause asked for a directed verdict of acquittal.

"There has been expert testimony, which is undisputed as far as any other expert testimony goes, that the defendant could not form a specific intent at the time of the shooting," Krause argued. "That being a necessary element for first-degree murder and the testimony being undisputed by the Commonwealth, I would ask that the first-degree murder charge be dismissed. As for the other charges, I believe that the defense of self-defense has been properly raised before the court."

"Denied," the judge said.

At nine-fifteen, fifteen minutes behind schedule, the jurors were led into the courtroom. "Ladies and gentlemen of the jury, we have been informed that there is no more testimony or evidence to be presented in this case," Judge Conway told them. "Now is the time for the attorneys to address their closing arguments to you."

Custom held that the defense argued first. Lee Krause, holding a legal pad scrawled with notes, stepped before the jury box and began by running through a witness-by-witness recapitulation of the trial. It was, for the most part, a dispassionate account. But he did attack the credibility of Jeanne Marie Coscia's story of the telephone conversation in which she said Glenn told her Travis had arrived at his apartment and "looks like he's gonna kick my ass."

Krause recalled Jeanne Marie's testimony that Glenn had asked her to call him back in an hour. "Jeanne Marie said she was tired and she went to sleep," Krause said. "She didn't call him back. She forgot to call him back. She then said that she never woke her mother up. She never woke anybody in the family up, even though she heard this. She didn't call anybody that night. The next day, she didn't say anything to her mother. And at school that morning she heard that Glenn had been shot. That is when she told somebody that she had this conversation. Not until then."

Beyond that, Krause repeatedly hammered at the issue of whether Travis had demonstrated a specific intent to kill. "We're looking at premeditated murder, malice aforethought," he said.

"That is an element in first-degree murder. In order for you to find Travis Umstadter guilty beyond a reasonable doubt of first-degree murder, you must find that the Commonwealth has proved to you all of the elements of the crime. And one of the elements is premeditation, malice aforethought, the specific intent to kill. If he could not form that specific intent, then you cannot convict him of first-degree murder. That is what the law is, whether you like it or don't like it. . . .

"The Commonwealth would have you believe that there was such intent because Travis said: 'Glenn won't live until spring. I wish he was dead. He hasn't suffered enough.' All of these statements don't go to intent, ladies and gentlemen. They go to motive. Don't be confused. Don't let the Commonwealth blow smoke at you to confuse you. Statements of that nature were made by every one of the folks that testified here [about Travis's threatening remarks]. They made them, too."

Krause said all those witnesses had motives similar to Travis's. "None of them had the specific intent to kill, including Travis," he argued. "Don't use statements made when Travis was drinking with friends—friends of both Travis and his sister

—to convict him. That is not the burden in this case at all. The test is could he form a specific intent at the time of this shooting to kill Glenn Evans."

As he had done at the beginning of the trial, Krause called the case "a tragedy—a terrible tragedy to this community, to this family." He said the Commonwealth undoubtedly would question why Travis had set the stage for that tragedy by going to Glenn's apartment in the first place.

"Why did he have the gun?" Krause asked. "Because he got nerve enough to go up there. Stupid thing. He's twenty years old. Pretty dumb. You can't convict him for going up there. You can't convict him for being drunk. He's not charged with that. What you have got to convict him for if you convict him is the cold-blooded murder of Glenn Evans."

But, of course, Krause urged the jurors not to convict. "You promised throughout the case to give this man a fair trial," he said. "I sincerely believed that you would listen only to the evidence from this witness stand, judge this man only on the evidence that was given, and apply the law as the court gives it to you. I'm telling you that those facts that you heard and the law the judge is going to give you leave no other decision and no other choice than to acquit this defendant of all charges."

When Ray Hamill got his turn, he came out firing. "The Commonwealth contends that this was a malicious killing," he said. "There were four gunshot wounds to the head. Three penetrated the brain stem. One penetrated the length of the brain. He was dead almost instantaneously. And yet there were four shots put into Glenn Evans's head and neck with a single-action revolver. The Commonwealth contends, ladies and gentlemen, that that is malicious intent."

Hamill argued that the evidence showed Travis was not so drunk he lacked the ability to form criminal intent. The prosecutor recounted the testimony of those who had spent time with Travis the night of the shooting—among them Dougie Smith and the witnesses who had been at the Mountain View bar. "To a person and without exception, they testified he wasn't intoxicated," Hamill said. "He could sit on the barstool.

He could play the jukebox. He could carry on a conversation. He could drive his car."

Then, the DA noted, Travis was able to find his way to Glenn's apartment. "He went exactly where he wanted to go. He intended to go to the apartment. He went to the apartment. Even by his own testimony, he had a thought process. He knew what he wanted to do. He knew how to achieve an end."

But the most graphic evidence of Travis's ability to function, by Hamill's account, was the actual firing of the shots. He recalled state police ballistic expert Wayne Poust's demonstration of how the single-action revolver worked.

"You pull the hammer back," Hamill said. "Then you pull the trigger. Bang! Hammer, trigger. Hammer, trigger. This isn't a semi-automatic weapon where you pull the trigger back and four shots get fired. There are eight separate steps involved in shooting this gun, putting four separate bullets in the head of Glenn Evans. Not only did he have the ability to go through the eight steps, but he had a marksmanship beyond repute. This defendant put four shots in the head and neck of a young man—one in the eye, one in the neck, and two behind the left ear."

Travis was not overpowered by alcohol, the DA argued. "He didn't kill because he drank. He drank in order to kill."

As for the self-defense claim, Hamill contended that even if Travis's story of the scissors attack were true—which the Commonwealth did not concede—Travis could easily have fled the apartment instead of shooting Glenn. "Think of the steps the defendant went through before he shot," Hamill said.

. "According to his testimony, a swipe is taken at him. Reflex action back. Then he steps out of the chair. He must then remember: I have a gun on me. He must then reach underneath [his outer shirt], pull out the gun, aim the gun, pull the hammer, and pull the trigger. Those are the steps he had to go through. Ladies and gentlemen, I suggest to you there was more than enough time for him to get out of that apartment. He was on his feet before he pulled that gun out. He could have turned and run right out of that apartment. But instead of exercising the opportunity to leave the apartment, he chose to pull the gun."

In response to Lee Krause's attacks on Jeanne Marie Coscia's credibility, Hamill argued that Jeanne Marie's account of her phone conversation with Glenn coincided with other evidence. Unless Jeanne Marie had talked to Glenn, Hamill asked, how would she have known what time Travis arrived at the apartment? "He says he was there from twelve-thirty to one o'clock," Hamill said. "That's what she says. How could she have possibly guessed twelve-thirty to one for his arrival unless it actually occurred?"

Recalling Travis's comment that Glenn would be "dead by spring," Hamill said it was more than an idle remark. "Why spring?" the DA asked. "Because Glenn was likely to be in jail by spring. And there would go the defendant's opportunity. His opportunity would be gone by springtime. If he was going to kill him, he had to do it by then."

The motive for the killing, Hamill said, was obvious. "It was revenge. It was revenge that led the defendant to say what he said about killing him by springtime. It was revenge that led him to drive down One-Ninety-One and go to Glenn's apartment. It was revenge that led him to conclude he should take the gun with him. It was revenge that led him into putting four gunshots from a single-action revolver in the head of Glenn Evans."

Hamill paused a moment before delivering his final words. "The defendant picked the date, the time, and the place for this execution," he said. "The defendant, by his acts, has picked his own verdict."

All that was left before the case went to the jury was for Judge Conway to deliver his charge. After offering the jurors still another review of the testimony, the judge explained their options to them.

To convict Travis of first-degree murder, they would have to agree on four elements: that Glenn was dead, that Travis killed him, that the crime was carried out with specific intent to kill, and that it was done with malice.

If the jurors decided all the elements were present except the specific intent to kill, they could convict Travis of third-degree murder. (Second-degree murder was not an option in the case.)

If the jurors found no persuasive evidence of malice, they could convict Travis of voluntary manslaughter. "Thus, if you find that Travis Umstadter sincerely but unreasonably believed it necessary to shoot Glenn Evans in order to protect himself, you may return a verdict of voluntary manslaughter," the judge said.

And, of course, the jury could find Travis not guilty on all counts.

John London, the retired airline maintenance manager serving as the lone remaining alternate juror, was now excused by Judge Conway. After devoting a week of his life to the case, London would not be permitted to join in the deliberations. "As you know, we did use one alternate," the judge told him a trifle apologetically. "We didn't use two, though."

At 12:50 P.M. on Monday, August 10, the twelve other jurors filed from the courtroom to begin pondering what was to become of Travis Umstadter.

THIRTEEN

Paintings of George Washington and Abraham Lincoln adorn the walls of the jury room in Wayne County Courthouse, just down the hall from Judge Robert Conway's chambers. But aside from those two concessions to the eye, the room seems purely functional.

Two tables are pushed together to afford the jurors a working space. Twelve brown wooden chairs—no more, no fewer—are set around the tables. Overhead are standard, bureaucratic-issue fluorescent lights. Inside the room are entrances to men's and women's lavatories for use solely by the jurors. Against one wall stands a small table bearing a coffee-brewing machine.

When the jury in Travis Umstadter's case withdrew to these working quarters to begin deliberations, retired insurance executive James Doherty assumed the powers of foreman strictly on the basis of seniority. He had been the first juror chosen. Doherty immediately took a preliminary sounding, asking where each juror stood at that moment.

There was a three-way split. Several jurors, the most vocal of them women, insisted that Travis should be convicted of first-degree murder. The thrust of their argument was: "We can't have young guys running around Wayne County shooting people." One male juror wanted a not-guilty verdict on all counts. He contended Travis shot Glenn Evans in self-defense—that Travis's account of the scissors attack rang true to him. But most of the jurors favored conviction on a third-degree-murder charge, chiefly on the ground that the Commonwealth had failed to prove premeditation.

Doherty and his fellow jurors set out to try to find some common ground. They talked for two hours. Then, at 2:50

P.M., they sent a note to the judge saying they needed further guidance.

Back in the courtroom, they asked him to redefine first-degree murder and third-degree murder and also to define malice. Judge Conway again told them first-degree murder required a specific intent to kill and malice.

"Now, a killing is with specific intent to kill if it is willful, deliberate, and premeditated," he said. "You will note that, although a defendant must premeditate it in order to have a specific intent to kill, premeditation does not require planning or previous thought. Premeditation can be very brief. All that is necessary is that it be time enough so the defendant intends to kill and is conscious of that intention."

After reviewing the definition of third-degree murder, Conway moved on to malice. He said a killing was regarded as carried out with malice if the killer showed an intent to kill or inflict serious bodily harm "or a wickedness of disposition, hardness of heart, cruelty, recklessness of consequences . . . and extreme indifference to the value of human life."

The jurors went back and talked for another hour, but returned to the courtroom at 4:00 P.M. to ask for a further explanation of how voluntary manslaughter differed from murder. Judge Conway drew the distinctions between the two crimes under Pennsylvania law, then sent the jury back to work.

Now it was five thirty-five. The jurors sent word they had a verdict.

All the players in the case were summoned to the courtroom. Travis was seated at the defense table with Lee Krause. Ray Hamill was at the Commonwealth's table. Travis's wife, mother, and father were huddled in the spectators' section, as were Glenn Evans's father and brothers. Judge Conway was on the bench, the jurors in their box.

Yet, after all the time this case had taken, there were at least a few who would later confess they were not yet ready to hear a verdict. The prospect—not only for Travis and his loved ones but for the community as well—seemed too awesome to contemplate. Like it or not, however, the time had come.

"Ladies and gentlemen of the jury, have you reached a verdict?" the judge asked.

"Yes, sir," James Doherty replied.

"Would you give the verdict slip to the clerk?" The clerk walked over and took the written verdict from Doherty.

"Would the foreman please read the verdict?"

"Charge Number One, murder in the first degree, we find the defendant not guilty," Doherty said.

Travis, his left hand cupping his chin and a blank expression on his face, showed no sign of animation.

"Charge Number Two, murder in the third degree, we find the defendant guilty."

Travis's face was still a mask. His parents held their emotions in check. But Chrissy broke into sobs.

Krause asked that the jury be polled. Each juror, in turn, affirmed that Travis had been found guilty of third-degree murder. Since that was so, a verdict on the charge of voluntary manslaughter became moot.

The judge directed Travis to stand. He explained that Travis could appeal the verdict but must file notice of appeal within ten days. Krause said he would do so.

Travis had not yet heard all of it. Judge Conway ordered all the spectators to leave the courtroom. He had the option of permitting Travis to remain free on bail during the appeal or of jailing him instantly.

Once the hubbub in the spectators' section had died, Judge Conway announced: "Bail is revoked. The sheriff is directed to take charge of the prisoner, to be remanded to the Wayne County Prison."

Judge Conway provided no explanation from the bench for his decision to imprison Travis immediately, but later would offer a rationale: "The fact that he was facing a maximum sentence of ten to twenty years significantly increased the risk of flight. Further, this was a tragic case . . . motivated by revenge. The families of all the parties continued to reside in the area, creating a situation which posed a potential danger to the defendant and others within the community."

The court proceedings were over by five forty-five. Sheriff's officers snapped handcuffs on Travis's wrists. Two deputies, each holding him by an arm, took him from the courtroom for the short walk through the courthouse parking lot to the prison. The expressionless mask had fled Travis's face. By now he was crying openly.

His parents left the courthouse with arms around each other, making their way through a cluster of reporters and photographers. The news media from Wayne County and nearby cities had given Travis's case extensive coverage. Although there were no television crews, still photographers, or sketch artists in the courtroom, the Umstadters had complained that the coverage was nonetheless oppressive. Laraine had collected a thick stack of newspaper clippings she described as either inaccurate or biased against Travis. Thus, as she and Dave walked down the courthouse steps with the guilty verdict fresh in their ears, their animosity toward the press suddenly burst loose. Each continuing to walk with an arm stretched across the other's back, Laraine and Dave used their free arms to fling angry gestures at the press.

Glenn Evans's brother Mark was standing outside the courthouse. He said of Travis and his family: "We're not violent like them. We'll just get on with our lives." Glenn's father, John Evans, said: "Twelve jurors made the decision. They have to live with their verdict. I have to live with the loss of my son. No verdict would have changed that."

At the county prison, Travis was locked into one of the six-by-ten cells whose brief acquaintance he had made immediately after his initial arrest. He was now in the custody of Sheriff William Bluff, a barrel-chested lawman who had been a state policeman for thirty-three years before taking over the sheriff's office in 1979. Bluff would find Travis "a regular prisoner—no problem at all."

Travis was obliged to wait more than five weeks before discovering the price he would have to pay for killing Glenn Evans. He spent much of the time reading in his cell. Although it seemed out of keeping with the image he projected, Travis was an avid reader. What he read, though, was more consistent with that image—a steady diet of Westerns.

At last, on September 17, Travis returned to Judge Conway's court for sentencing. The maximum sentence would be ten to twenty years in state prison. As Ray Hamill noted at the outset of the sentencing proceedings, Pennsylvania imposed a mandatory minimum sentence of five years for any third-degree murder committed with a firearm.

"Your Honor, it should come as no surprise to anyone who knows the position that the Commonwealth has taken in this case that we will be asking the court to impose a maximum sentence," Hamill said.

"The Commonwealth prosecuted this case on evidence it believed justified a first-degree-murder conviction, which the Commonwealth readily acknowledges was not rendered but rather murder in the third degree. The prosecution was based on a crime that would have carried a mandatory life sentence had the first-degree conviction been obtained."

Ever since the accident that killed Kristen Umstadter, Hamill said, there had been a tendency in the community to stigmatize certain young people involved in that case and the events that followed. "I don't think that is fair," Hamill told the judge.

"We have young adults here who have frailties as well as human strengths. In no way, shape, or form do I intend to pigeonhole the defendant in this case. What I do look to, Your Honor, is the evidence in the case.

"We have a crime that was committed by placing four gunshots into the head and neck of a twenty-year-old man. Shots fired from close range from a single-action revolver with deadly accuracy bespeaking an execution."

Hamill recalled Travis's claims that he acted in self-defense and did not even remember firing the second, third, and fourth shots. "Your Honor, the Commonwealth does not believe that," the DA said.

"We find it incredible that he doesn't remember a second, third, and fourth shot, but remembers the first shot and remembers leaving there and going home. We find it incredible that he still claims he acted in self-defense when the evidence is clearly inconsistent with that and the jury emphatically rejected self-defense. . . .

"The crime has all the markings of an eye for an eye and a tooth for a tooth. It has all the markings of the defendant taking the law into his own hands. It evidenced a hardness of heart such as I have not seen as district attorney. I said to the jury in my opening, Your Honor, that Glenn Evans was awaiting sentence on the charges arising out of the fateful automobile accident. I submit to the court that the defendant imposed the sentence in that case. I don't believe that the defendant showed Glenn Evans any mercy or mitigation whatsoever.

"The Commonwealth would ask that the court fairly and justly consider all the factors involved in this case. The Commonwealth would ask the court to impose the maximum sentence."

Travis remained silent at the sentencing, leaving it to Lee Krause to do all the talking on his behalf. "Your Honor, I both opened and closed this case by calling it a tragedy," Krause said.

"It is a tragedy for my client most of all, for his family secondly, for the community thirdly, and for the country as a whole. It has gotten more attention than any case I have ever been involved in. I submit, Your Honor, that it got that attention, and continues to get that attention, because it is a tragedy.

"It was not the type of crime where there was a killing that was absolutely nonsensical. This was a killing resulting from a car crash in which the defendant's sister suffered and died. I believe there was evidence that the defendant, this youth, was psychologically disturbed to a great degree."

Krause argued that Travis had not only suffered the grief shared by the entire Umstadter family but also had endured additional pressure because of his parents' dependence on him to find answers to their questions about Kristen's death. "That doesn't excuse his act," Krause said.

"It doesn't excuse anything at all. What happened that night in attempting to find out the truth from Glenn Evans, and talking to him, resulted in a tragedy—a terrible tragedy. But I keep in mind that this young man does not have any prior criminal record. This man does not rob gas stations, stick up people, beat up anybody. He's never gone to jail before. He has never been before a court in his life. He is twenty years old. He had witnesses testify in court as to his truthfulness.

"Your Honor, from the day this event happened all the way through, I have lived an awful long time with this case. I submit to you that this young man is deserving of mitigation with regard to this sentence. To impose the maximum sentence would compound the tragedy, continue the tragedy, both for my client and his family. No amount of incarceration is going to bring back either of the two lives which are lost. No amount of incarceration is going to correct any problems with this young man. This young man is not a murderer. This young man does not go out and commit crimes. This young man is not a danger to society.

"This young man needs help and he has been seeking help. He has been seeing a psychiatrist. But he does not need the punishment to be so severe as to compound this tragedy. I would ask Your Honor to look at his good record, look at the special and significant circumstances of this case, and *not*, Your Honor, *not* to impose the full extent of the law in this case."

Judge Conway said he had reviewed a nine-page report on Travis's background prepared by probation officer Linus Myers. "It is favorable to the defendant," the judge said.

"The evidence in this case that is most important is the fact that the defendant went in late at night to the victim's apartment and, after a time with a loaded gun, fired four shots into his body. One into the eye, one into the neck, and two behind the ear. Each capable of killing him. A person has to be responsible for his own acts.

"It has been mentioned that there is a tragedy here. The tragedy is that there is a murder here. After I impose sentence, and at the completion of the sentence, the defendant will have a life to lead. The victim here has no life to lead.

"I feel that the facts of the crime itself demand that justice in this case be best served by giving the maximum sentence prescribed by law—that Travis Umstadter be incarcerated for a period of not less than ten years nor more than twenty years."

Travis shuddered and broke into muffled sobs. His wife, seated behind him, lowered her head and struggled for control. Krause was on his feet, telling the judge he would shortly file an appeal. Pending the appeal's outcome, Krause asked Conway to order that Travis remain in Wayne County Prison—rather than being sent directly into the state prison system.

"That is not my policy in this court," the judge said. "Motion is denied."

Thus, after meeting with his family for an emotional farewell, Travis was taken to Graterford State Prison near Philadelphia—a reception and classification center for the prison system. It was to be only a temporary stay, intended to indoctrinate Travis to prison life and determine where he should serve the balance of his sentence.

The prison authorities, after evaluating both Travis and his crime, sent him to Rockview State Prison at Bellefonte in central Pennsylvania. Rockview, built in 1912, was designed to hold a maximum of 1,250 inmates but now accommodated close to two thousand. Classified as a medium-security prison, Rockview nonetheless was regarded by convicts as a tough "joint"—a characterization no doubt abetted by its designation as the site of Pennsylvania's electric chair. Beginning in 1915, there had been 350 executions at Rockview. And, although the electric chair had gone unused since 1962 because of legal and political conflicts over the death penalty, there were now more than a hundred Pennsylvania inmates under death sentences, and pressure was building to resume capital punishment.

Rockview sat high on a hill overlooking State Highway 26. It offered an imposing sight—with two enormous cellblocks, holding half of the prison population between them, looming ominously before passing travelers. The other inmates were spread among smaller buildings at the thirty-acre institution, which was ringed by fifteen-foot fences crowned with razor-ribbon wire. Gun towers were spotted strategically around the perimeter.

Inmates who qualified were permitted to leave their cells for varying lengths of time from 6:30 A.M. to 9:00 P.M. Their time outside the cells was spent on jobs in vocational shops and a cannery, on studies in the prison's education buildings, and on recreational activities.

Travis Umstadter did not, by any means, adjust well to prison life. Usually murderers are considered the prison elite. But Travis saw no great honor in his criminal status. He sank into a dark depression. He suffered a radical weight loss. His hair started to fall out in clumps. He cried uncontrollably at times. His parents tried to get him psychiatric help, without success.

To make matters worse, there were periodic outbreaks of violence at the prison. One day, a small riot erupted in the mess hall—apparently instigated by a convict angered over being punished for misconduct. Eleven guards and a handful of prisoners were injured in the fracas. Although Travis was not hurt, that incident and others exacerbated his depression.

Every weekend, Laraine Umstadter and her young daughter-in-law, Chrissy, drove the 350-mile round trip to Rockview to visit Travis. Try as they might, they could rarely draw an upbeat word from him. "The biggest thing he was dealing with even then was Kristen's death," Laraine would recall. "He didn't know how or why it happened. And then the other thing he was trying to deal with was: How could he get involved in something like this?"

The one measure of hope sustaining Travis and all the Umstadters was that his conviction might be reversed. Lee Krause was methodically pursuing the appeal. The case was now in the hands of the Superior Court of Pennsylvania, one level below the State Supreme Court. Krause filed a forty-one-page brief with the Superior Court, urging a reversal.

He contended that Judge Conway had committed sundry

errors in presiding over the trial—among them restricting Krause's re-creation of the confrontation between Travis and Glenn; failing to grant a mistrial after juror Patricia Watson's emotional outburst; limiting the scope of the defense's psychiatric testimony; refusing to grant Krause's motion for dismissal of the charges at the close of the Commonwealth's case; and failing to recognize that there was insufficient evidence to overturn Travis's self-defense claim. Beyond that, Krause accused Conway of "exhibiting bias" against Travis throughout the case and thus depriving him of a fair trial.

It was not until November 3, 1988, almost fourteen months after Travis entered prison, that the Superior Court heard arguments in his case. A three-judge panel was convened to consider the arguments in a spacious, handsomely paneled courtroom on the second floor of the old post office building at Ninth and Chestnut streets in Philadelphia. The courtroom's walls were decorated with photographs of county courthouses all over Pennsylvania. For some seemingly inexplicable reason, however, there was no picture of Wayne County Courthouse.

As was customary, Travis was not brought from prison to hear the arguments. But Laraine and Chrissy were there—both appearing jittery, Chrissy ducking out of the courtroom periodically for a smoke while other cases were being heard. Chrissy, her bright face shadowed by dark, sad eyes, was wearing a pink turtleneck sweater, a beige skirt, and a single strand of pearls. Laraine had chosen a beige blouse, a gray plaid jacket, and a beige skirt. When Travis's case was called, they settled into seats in the back row of the courtroom—leaning forward to hear the proceedings.

On the bench in their black robes were the three middle-aged men who might well decide how Travis would pass the years until his own middle age: Judge Patrick Tamilia, his black hair thinning, his glasses perched low on his nose; Judge Patrick Cavanaugh, ruddy and graying; and Judge Zoran Popovich, rugged, dark-haired, peering through gold-rimmed glasses.

Lee Krause and Ray Hamill—notes and briefs in hand—stepped to the front of the courtroom. Krause, wearing a gray suit with a gray tie, took the lectern before the bench. He began on familiar ground—speaking of the Umstadter family's tragedy.

"This family lost a daughter as a result of an automobile accident involving a drunk driver—the victim in the current case," Krause said. "There was a very close relationship between the defendant and his sister, Kristen. The family pressures placed on Travis were immense. The family mercilessly sought answers to questions about the death of his sister. There was a definite personality change in Travis—manifested most clearly in heavy drinking."

At the rear of the courtroom, Laraine and Chrissy were staring straight ahead. Their faces were expressionless.

Krause then began a review of the errors he contended Judge Conway had committed during the trial—each of which he claimed entitled Travis to a reversal of the conviction. He started with juror Patricia Watson's outburst.

"I asked for a mistrial," Krause said. "The outburst most certainly had some effect on the other jurors. One other juror thought this juror was banging her head against a wall. But the judge denied my motion for a mistrial. I cannot see how the trial could continue any further."

Judge Tamilia asked: "Isn't that within the province of the judge to decide?"

"Yes," Krause conceded. "But I believe he had a duty to declare a mistrial."

When Krause argued that Conway also erred in denying the defense motion for dismissal of the charges at the close of the Commonwealth's case, Judge Cavanaugh told him the Superior Court did not have authority to review that issue. Krause moved on to Conway's ruling restricting the re-creation of the confrontation in Glenn's apartment. "The demonstration I attempted to conduct was halted not on a motion by the Commonwealth but by the judge," Krause said. "The scene was set for the demonstration. I don't think it was a surprise. But it was halted by the judge. Thereafter, the Commonwealth used the exact same table and chairs I was using and conducted a demonstration that went far beyond what I was prevented from doing. What's good for the goose is good for the gander."

On the self-defense issue, Krause contended Travis carried his gun into Glenn's apartment because "he knew the victim had a violent background." After recounting Travis's story of the scissors attack, Krause said: "He fired the gun."

"How many times?" Judge Tamilia asked.

"Four times, Your Honor."

"And this wasn't a gun that fired automatically?"

"No."

Krause also attacked Conway's decision restricting defense use of psychiatric testimony. "The testimony would have shown there was a mental defect on the part of the defendant," he argued. "Because of his state of mind, he was unable to consider retreat [from Glenn's apartment] as a course of conduct available to him. Testimony of this kind should have been admitted."

All these rulings and others, Krause said, were evidence of Conway's prejudice against Travis. "The bias of the judge was eminently apparent throughout the trial," he argued.

Ray Hamill, wearing a red tie with his gray suit, stepped to the lectern. He had already filed an extensive brief with the court rebutting Krause's arguments. Thus he delivered only a brief oral presentation.

On the juror's outburst, Hamill said: "The defense counsel was given ample opportunity to question that juror and her roommate. There is no evidence that this jury was prejudiced or tampered with in any way."

On the psychiatric testimony, Hamill noted that he had conceded it was proper for a psychiatrist to testify about Travis's intoxication on the night of the shooting. "But then defense counsel tried to make voluntary intoxification a justification for the defendant's acts," he said. "That's not the law."

Hamill argued that he had presented substantial evidence at the trial proving Travis's guilt. Therefore, he said, Judge Conway made the proper decision in denying Krause's motion for dismissal. Moreover, he contended, "the evidence presented throughout the course of the trial was sufficient" to overcome the defense claim of self-defense.

As for Krause's contention that Judge Conway had been prejudiced against Travis, Hamill said: "The trial judge conducted the trial in a fair and impartial manner and afforded the defendant all of his rights." In support of his argument, Hamill noted that at one point—in delivering his charge to the jury— Judge Conway had neglected to offer instructions on the law dealing with self-defense. When Krause pointed out the omission, Hamill said, Conway went back and gave the jurors the instructions Krause had requested.

Hamill closed his argument by urging the Superior Court to uphold Travis's conviction. "The bottom line is that the defendant went into the victim's home and fired four shots into the victim with his own gun," he said.

The appeals court took the case under advisement. Laraine and Chrissy went home to await an uneasy Thanksgiving and Christmas. When the Umstadters put up their Christmas tree, Laraine decorated it solely with yellow ribbons dedicated to Travis's early release. She also had tied yellow ribbons around the radio antenna of her beige Oldsmobile.

Nineteen days after Christmas, on January 13, 1989, the three Superior Court judges handed down a unanimous decision that systematically considered and then knocked down every contention on which Krause had hoped to reverse the conviction. "We reject all of appellant's arguments and affirm [the conviction]," the court ruled.

When word of the decision reached Honesdale, the Umstadters were devastated anew. They were so fearful of Travis's reaction that they did not tell him about the ruling for weeks.

One day, Lee Krause found in his mail a letter from Laraine Umstadter informing him that she was firing him as Travis's attorney. Krause telephoned her.

"Laraine, you can't fire me," he said. "You're not my client."

Now Laraine had no choice except to tell Travis of the Superior Court's decision. Travis, who had yet to adjust to prison life, sank into even deeper depression—but not so deep that he would fail to fulfill his mother's wishes. Soon afterward, Krause received another dismissal letter. This one was signed by Travis. The Umstadters then retained another lawyer, Paul Gettleman of Zelienople, Pennsylvania.

Gettleman appealed the case to the Pennsylvania Supreme Court, pressing the contention that Judge Conway had erred in limiting the psychiatric testimony at the trial. But lawyers familiar with the case considered it improbable, given the unequivocal Superior Court decision, that the case would be reversed and sent back to Honesdale for retrial.

Lee Krause, who knew the defense case better than anyone, took what he considered a realist's view. "That case is *never* coming back," he said.

Krause was right. On June 26, 1990, the Pennsylvania Supreme Court denied Travis's appeal without comment.

By that time, Travis was four months shy of his twenty-fourth birthday. And he was still looking at seven to seventeen years remaining to be served in a state prison where he claimed he did not belong.

FOURTEEN

"There were no bad people involved in this whole story," school administrator Dan O'Neill says. "Maybe that's what makes it the greatest tragedy of all."

O'Neill is leaning forward in his chair, his hands folded across the top of his desk. "These were all good kids," he says. "Yes, Glenn and Travis drank too much beer and drank it illegally. But does that make them delinquents? I don't think so. They weren't bad. And Kristen certainly wasn't bad. She was a lovely girl."

At least one benefit did accrue, O'Neill says, from all the shock and sorrow that descended on Honesdale. "There's less drinking and driving," he says. "Kids still drink at parties. But they make sure someone who doesn't drink is going to drive."

Perhaps. There still is not much, however, for young people to do in Honesdale. And at least some of them still can be seen cruising—beer bottles in hand—to pass the time.

Dougie Smith is sitting in a booth at the Towne House Diner, glancing out the window at the traffic crawling by on Main Street. Dougie has changed jobs since Travis's trial and now is working for a General Motors dealer. He is a wearing a mechanic's uniform jacket with his name stitched across the pocket.

"Travis was my best friend," he says softly. "I went all the way through school with him. We did everything together. After the shooting, there was a lot of heat on me because I was in the car that night with Travis. I talked to Travis and he told me to tell the truth. And I would have told the truth anyway. But, after I did, Travis got furious with me. He won't have anything to do with me anymore. I stayed on good terms with his parents. But when my parents wrote Travis a letter in prison, he said he didn't want to have anything to do with me or my family. As I say, he told me to tell the truth. But maybe he didn't remember how much I knew."

After he testified against Travis, Dougie says, some of their friends also turned antagonistic toward him. "They said there were things I didn't have to tell," Dougie says. "There were threats against me and my family. But I was just doing what I thought was right."

By chance, on another day, the same seat in the diner is occupied by Allan Rutledge. Although the memorabilia of his romance with Kristen remain stored away, Allan says he still is unable to put her behind him. "She was everything I ever wanted," he says. "I can't get her out of my mind."

Allan, who once nurtured an abiding hatred for Glenn Evans and anyone associated with him, now concedes he has mellowed a trifle—but only a trifle. He is working as a house framer. Occasionally, supplies are delivered to his job site by Glenn's brother Mark, who works for a local lumberyard. "We've gotten to the point where we can say, 'How you doing?'" Allan says. "But that's about it."

Glenn's mother, Eva Furk, confined to her home by her paralysis, is lying in bed in a small ranch house surrounded by thick woods across the state line in Cochecton, New York. She is a tiny woman with gray hair, a lined face, and a thick German accent. When she was fifteen, she fled her native East Germany with a girlfriend. She later made her way to the United States and now has been here for twenty-seven years.

"I cry for Glenn all the time," she says. "I miss him so. Everything went against him for his whole life. It's agonizing."

Glenn was "a good boy," she says. "He liked cars, he liked girls, and he liked food. He liked all kinds of food, but cereal the most. And he liked to cook. He could cook anything." Furk describes Glenn's ambitions as simple. "All he ever wanted to do was be a mechanic."

As for Travis, she insists the courts let him off easy—that he should have been convicted of first-degree murder. "For him to take revenge on Glenn this way, that's what makes me so angry. He should be in jail for the rest of his life. He should never be let loose on society."

Even some regarded as friends of Travis are reluctant to defend him. Sherry Dennis is standing behind the bar at the Mountain View in a bright pink minidress. "I like Travis," she says. "But what he did was wrong. You can't take an eye for an eye."

Ray Hamill takes a broader view of the events. Sitting behind his desk in the DA's office at the courthouse, Hamill says, "This was a trial in the courtroom and it was a trial for the community."

Laraine Umstadter no longer works as a legal secretary. She says she soured on the law by seeing "how the system works" in the cases involving her children. Now, she sells real estate.

Sitting at a conference table in a Century 21 office south of Honesdale, Laraine is asked how life is treating her. "To use my least favorite word, it sucks," she says. "I hate that word. But that's how it is. It sucks."

Travis, she says, is still struggling with prison life. "He doesn't think anybody is going to help or understand. After Kristen's death, Travis went through a horrible anger. It must have been terrible. I thought he might beat Glenn up, but I never thought he'd do what he did. He's not bad. I don't condone what he did, but I certainly understand."

Despite the passage of time, Laraine still is driven by the conviction that her family has suffered all manner of injustices at the hands of fate, the police, the courts, the press, and society at large. She argues, for instance, that Travis's sentence was inconsistent with other sentences handed down by Judge Robert Conway. One case she cites involves a teenager who shot his father to death with clear premeditation. Conway sentenced him to a lesser term than Travis's—seven to fourteen years.

Asked why Judge Conway or anyone else would have had it in for Travis, Laraine concedes: "I don't know why."

She is just as protective of Kristen in death as she is of Travis in prison, insisting that the stories told at Glenn's trial inspired the press and some in the community to try to tarnish Kristen's memory. "I still believe Kristen was coaxed into Glenn's car," Laraine says. "I'll never believe that her death was her fault."

Dave Umstadter has sold his general store. Before Travis went on trial, his family acquired a tractor-trailer in the hope that he would remain free and be able to make a living driving the rig. Now it is Dave who drives the rig—hauling loads to California and back.

Crisscrossing the country, alone in a tractor-trailer cab, offers a man an abundance of time to think. Dave spends much of his time brooding over the calamities that have befallen his family. One day, during a stop in Denver, he determines to vent at least some of his anger and frustration. He scribbles off a letter to the editor of a small Wayne County newspaper—a letter meant not for publication but rather to offer the editor an insight into the Umstadters' feelings.

"I am writing this letter from the cab of my truck, so I ask you to forgive the poor spelling," Dave begins.

"Kristen was the finest young lady I ever knew—Sunday-school teacher, camp counselor, homecoming queen, etc. She didn't drink or smoke or do drugs, and she was not a wild partier. The investigation of the accident that killed her was appallingly shoddy, as is the case in all drunk-driving accidents in Wayne County. It is the sort of thing that prominent law-and-order Honesdale citizens like to sweep under the rug.

"Glenn Evans was, by one police officer's description, 'a maniac behind the wheel.' Glenn Evans never made any attempt to say he was sorry. Instead, he went out doing the same things—laughing, saying 'the dumb bitch got what she deserved' and that nothing was going to happen to him. Travis and all of us knew what was going on.

"Travis was having a very hard time with the loss of his sister, going to the cemetery and crying and carrying on terribly. . . . Every day is still hard for my wife and I. She has suffered terribly with depression and stress. At times I've been unable to work. Yet we're considered such horrible people and Glenn Evans is a folk hero."

Alluding to the old stigma attached to "transplants" by some Honesdale natives, Dave attributes Travis's maximum sentence to an attempt by Judge Conway "to teach those outsiders a lesson." He writes that he can never accept that sentence as fair. "I am so bitter that I would gladly leave this country forever if I could gain my son's freedom."

At the apartment where Travis fired the four bullets into Glenn's head, the door is opened by a young man named Aron Timur. He rented the apartment after Mark Evans moved elsewhere. The blood stains are long gone, and there is nothing in the apartment to hint at what the walls might say if they could speak of what actually transpired here.

"I knew when I moved in that this was where the murder happened," Timur says. "It doesn't bother me, even though I went to school with Glenn. I kept waiting during the trial for people to knock at the door—wanting to see the place—but nobody ever came."

At the place where it all began, out there on Highway 652 between Honesdale and Beach Lake, it appears the pines and hemlocks off in the distance have grown a couple of feet since that August night when Glenn Evans's Duster skidded into the path of V. A. Conrad's station wagon. Aside from that, only one change in the scene is evident. As a warning to motorists, the state police have painted a yellow circle on the pavement to mark the precise spot where Kristen Umstadter died.

At Honesdale High School, a memorial fund named for Kristen is used to buy equipment not otherwise available. At her grave behind the Lookout United Methodist Church, a gentle breeze drifts one afternoon through the old cemetery. A pumpkin and a basket of fresh red, orange, and white tulips stand before the headstone attesting that "to know her was to love her."

But these are not the sole memorials to Kristen Umstadter and to the cataclysm her death precipitated. There is at least one more. It is currently on view at Rockview State Prison. It is on Travis's arm—a tattoo acquired after his imprisonment. The tattoo bears a picture of a cross accompanied by four words:

REST IN PEACE, SISTER.

ACKNOWLEDGMENTS

It often seems I've spent half my life descending without invitation on some unsuspecting town to write a story townsfolk did not particularly want told—no matter how urgently it needed telling. This story was cut from the familiar pattern.

Yet with only a few exceptions, the people of Honesdale and Wayne County proved uncommonly hospitable and cooperative to an outlander bent on poking into deep wounds and resurrecting events they were eager to put behind them. I am grateful to them all.

District Attorney Ray Hamill and defense attorney Lee Krause showed eternal patience and good humor in making time again and again to talk to me. Members of the Umstadter and Evans families, although far from ecstatic about seeing such a book written, provided valuable contributions.

Among others who made their own contributions:

In the Pennsylvania State Police: Sergeant John Brostowski, criminal investigator Herman Todd, and troopers Robert Fuehrer, Andrew Piezga, and Michael O'Day, all at the Honesdale barracks; and Tom Lyon at State Police headquarters in Harrisburg.

In the Honesdale school system: Superintendent of Schools Dan O'Neill and guidance counselor Carl Cerar.

At Wayne County Courthouse: prothonotary J. Edmund Rose and his entire staff, especially Joan Shaffer and Linda Soden, who gave me a place to work during interminable examinations of court records and who hunted down a seemingly endless succession of documents for me; Linus Myers, the chief county probation officer; and Vincent Scamell, administrator of the local courts. And nearby, at Wayne County Prison, Sheriff William Bluff.

The lawyers in the Glenn Evans trial: defense attorney Bob Bryan and prosecutor Mark Zimmer.

In the local press: Kristen Ammerman-Scofield, managing editor of the *Wayne Independent;* her father, Clifford Ammerman, a former editor of the *Independent* and a rich mine of information on the community; J. W. Johnson, another former *Independent* editor; and Jim Dyson, editor of the *News Eagle,* published in nearby Hawley, Pennsylvania.

At Rockview State Prison: Jack Allar of the correction superintendent's staff.

Also, Dr. Young W. Lee, the county coroner; James J. Doherty, foreman of the jury in Travis Umstadter's murder trial; Allan Rutledge; Doug Smith; Jeanne Marie Coscia; Mark Ordnung; Dawn Miller; Elwin Ostrander; V. A. Conrad; Sherry Dennis; Clinton Dennis; Fred Chalmers; Aron Timur; Kelly Vinton White; Debbie Robbins; Bruce Cassidy at the Superior Court of Pennsylvania in Philadelphia; and the executive staff of Excam, Inc., of Hialeah, Florida, manufacturer of the single-action pistol that killed Glenn Evans.

I am indebted to my agent, Philippa Brophy, and to my editors, Brian DeFiore and E. J. McCarthy, for faith, patience, and counsel.

As always, I am grateful for the opportunity to thank my wife, Jeanne, for enduring the rigors of life in a writer's household. Our older daughter, Pamela G. Dorman, who views the publishing world from an editor's inside perspective, was a frequent source of good advice about the book. Our younger daughter, Patricia German, who views the publishing world with the detachment of an outsider, was a frequent source of good advice about the world at large.